普通高等学校经管类精品教材

外贸函电

主　　编　孙金琳　张　芳
副主编　王晶晶　张　冬　朱　振
编写人员（以姓氏笔画为序）
　　　　　王　斌　王晶晶　朱　振
　　　　　孙金琳　汪雅雪　张　冬
　　　　　张　芳　杨玉春

中国科学技术大学出版社

内 容 简 介

本书精选和提炼了国际商务函电所涉及的重要内容,把传授商务基本知识与训练函电写作技能融为一体,介绍了外贸关系建立的全过程,包含外贸业务磋商过程中各个环节往来函电:建立业务关系、询盘与发盘、还盘、达成交易、开立与修改信用证、装运、保险、收款、索赔及理赔等,旨在使学生掌握外贸各个环节的写作技巧,为步入工作岗位奠定基础。

图书在版编目(CIP)数据

外贸函电/孙金琳,张芳主编. —合肥:中国科学技术大学出版社,2020.8
ISBN 978-7-312-05000-8

Ⅰ.外… Ⅱ.①孙… ②张… Ⅲ.对外贸易—英语—电报信函—写作—高等学校—教材 Ⅳ.F75

中国版本图书馆 CIP 数据核字(2020)第 148721 号

外贸函电
WAIMAO HANDIAN

出版	中国科学技术大学出版社
	安徽省合肥市金寨路96号,230026
	http://press.ustc.edu.cn
	https://zgkxjsdxcbs.tmall.com
印刷	安徽省瑞隆印务有限公司
发行	中国科学技术大学出版社
经销	全国新华书店
开本	787 mm×1092 mm 1/16
印张	15
字数	384 千
版次	2020 年 8 月第 1 版
印次	2020 年 8 月第 1 次印刷
定价	40.00 元

Preface
前　　言

随着世界经济一体化和全球化进程的发展,国与国之间的经济联系越来越密切,国际贸易在经济中的地位不断提高,这也使得我国在发展国民经济的过程中需要大量的国际贸易人才。熟练运用外贸英语函电是国际经济贸易专业人才的职业核心素养,因此外贸英语函电课程也是国际贸易相关专业人才培养的核心课程。为切实提高我国国际贸易专业人才的商务英语函电运用能力,本书编写团队从高职教学的特点和培养目标出发,将多年从事外贸英语函电的教学经验和商务实践相结合,组织编写了本书。

本书是一本介绍外贸英语信函写作基本内容及提高学习者外贸函电写作技能的实用性教材,分为八个模块,系统介绍了商务英语函电写作基本知识、业务磋商、交易的达成、备货阶段沟通、货物出运前后沟通、卖方收款、索赔及理赔、其他日常工作等函电写作内容。

本书内容新颖、体系完整、实用性强。每个单元内容都包含了导入、背景知识介绍、例信、注释、课后练习等部分。与同类教材相比,本书除重点编录外贸业务磋商过程中各个环节往来函电的实例,例如:建立业务关系、询盘与发盘、还盘、达成交易、开立与修改信用证、装运、保险、收款、索赔及理赔等环节,同时也增设了其他相关日常工作的函电写作,如出差自动回复、休假通知、职务调动通知、展会安排通知以及节日问候函电,增强了教材的实用性。相关教师可扫描以下二维码登录安徽省网络课程学习中心("e会学"),或者下载"e会学"APP,进入孙金琳老师主讲的"外贸函电"课程,查看相关课程知识点的MOOC视频,理解教学难点,巩固教学重点,从而提高教材使用效果,增加教材的趣味性和实用性。

安徽省网络课程学习中心二维码

"e会学"APP二维码

本书编写人员为高等院校外贸函电课程的一线教师及相关企业人员,体现了工学结合的特色,能够充分保证内容的专业性。本书由芜湖职业技术学院孙金琳策划,由孙金琳、张芳审校全稿并担任主编,芜湖职业技术学院王晶晶、张冬、朱振担任副主编,安徽商贸职业技术学院汪雅雪、合肥沙曼拉电子商务有限公司总经理王斌和芜湖昊轩环保新材料有限公司外贸经理杨玉春参编。孙金琳编写第三单元和第六单元,张芳编写第一单元和第九单元,王晶晶编写第四单元和第十二单元,张冬编写第五单元和第八单元,朱振编写第二单元和第十单元,汪雅雪编写第七单元和第十一单元,王斌和杨玉春参与教材大纲的制定,并提供了部分真实案例。

  本书在编写的过程中参阅了大量国内外教材,参考文献未能一一列出,在此表示真诚的感谢!由于编者水平有限,书中难免有不足之处,恳请读者批评指正。

编 者

Contents
目　　录

Preface
前言 ·· (ⅰ)

Module 1　Basic Knowledge of Business English Letters Writing
商务英语函电写作基本知识 ··· (1)
　　Unit 1　Introduction to Business English Letters Writing ·················· (3)

Module 2　Business Negotiation
业务磋商 ·· (19)
　　Unit 2　Establishing Business Relations ··· (21)
　　Unit 3　Inquiry and Offer ·· (37)
　　Unit 4　Counter-offer ··· (64)

Module 3　Conclusion of Business
交易的达成 ··· (89)
　　Unit 5　Order and Contract ··· (91)

Module 4　Communication in Stage of Preparation of the Goods
备货阶段沟通 ··· (107)
　　Unit 6　Establishment and Amendment of L/C ································ (109)

Module 5　Communication before and after Shipment
货物出运前后沟通 ·· (133)
　　Unit 7　Shipment ·· (135)
　　Unit 8　Insurance ·· (156)

Module 6　The Receipt of Payment by the Seller
卖方收款 ·· (169)
　　Unit 9　Payment ·· (171)

Module 7   Claims and Settlement
索赔及理赔 ·· (189)
   Unit 10   Complaints, Claims and Settlement ································ (191)

Module 8   Other Routine Works
其他日常工作 ·· (209)
   Unit 11   Other Routine Letters ··· (211)
   Unit 12   Holiday Greetings ·· (221)

Reference
参考文献 ·· (234)

Module 1
Basic Knowledge of Business English Letters Writing
商务英语函电写作基本知识

Unit 1　Introdution to Business English Letters Writing
商务英语函电写作入门

Lead-in

Try to finish the following tasks and find out the learning objectives of this unit.

Task 1

宏发工艺品进出口公司的经理 Tony 发现,公司新进员工在开展业务时存在一个普遍问题,即在与客户进行外贸英文函电沟通时逻辑混乱、表达不清楚,写出的邮件不够专业。因此,他认为在开展业务之前,有必要对员工进行外贸英文函电写作基本知识的培训。请说出商务英语函电写作应遵循的原则,以及商务英语函电的组成部分。

Tastk 2

商务英语函电中日期的写法,应注意以下几点:
(1) 年份应写完整,不能简写。
(2) 月份要用英文表示,不要用数字代替。
(3) 具体日期可用基数词,也可用序数词。
(4) 英式英语中日期的表达顺序是日月年,美式英语中日期的表达顺序是月日年。日月和年份之间用逗号分开。
请写出"2020 年 7 月 1 日"的英文表达。

Part Ⅰ　Introduction

商务英语函电写作的基础是英语语言的运用能力、逻辑思维能力、对事物的分析和判断能力以及解决问题的实践能力。因此,要写好商务英语函电首先要夯实语言基础,提高综合能力。就写作而言,商务英语函电有其自身的特点和要求:形式上,讲究行文格式,有比较固定的布局和写法;语言上,要求简洁、清楚、明了;内容上,要求真实、具体、准确、完整。商务函电不同于社交函电,无需嘘寒问暖,要开门见山,应该遵循简洁、明了、务实的原则。冗长或语义不明的语句会使对方失去耐心和兴趣,甚至会使公司失去业务发展的机会,从而蒙受损失。商务英语函电在内容的组织上有一定的格式可循。函电的正文通常可分为三部分:第一部分,提及对方来信,说明写信的目的;第二部分,针对对方函电所提问题,详细介绍情况或说明原因;第三部分,对未来对方应采取的行动表达期待。为了把复杂的业务内容用英语表达清楚,最好一个句子只表达一个意思,一个段落只表达一个话题,一封信只表达一个主题。在写商务函电之前,要考虑收信的对象。如果是不熟悉的部门或是第一次做生意的客户,就必须采取较正式的语气和形式,注意礼貌周到。若是写给熟悉的部门或客户,则可以采用较为平易近人的称呼和用词。

Part Ⅱ　Letter Writing Guide

This unit mainly introduces the basic knowledge of writing English correspondence for international trade, namely, principle, layout, format of business letters and structure of Emails.

The principle involves 5Cs that must be observed in writing effective business letters targeted at handling the business in question.

The layout section demonstrates to learners what constitutes a business letter and how these constituents are arranged to form an effective business letter.

The format section briefly introduces the format styles commonly adopted in writing business letter, namely, the indented style, full-block style and modified block style.

The email section deals with the composition of business emails, giving some tips on the details of each part of an email.

Part Ⅲ Basic Knowledge of Business English Letters

1. Principles of Business English Letters Writing

A well-structured business letter is the core of effective communication. To some extent, a good business letter is a good advertising of a company and can deliver the favorable image of company to the customers. Generally speaking, a business letter often follows the 5C Principles.

Correctness

Correctness is considered to be the most important principle.

Business letters must be correct, otherwise they may be misunderstood or lead to great loss to both exporters and importers. Usually business letters involve the rights, the duties and the interests of both sides.

Therefore, business letters must have factual information, accurate figures and exact terms with correct grammars, spellings and punctuation. Pay more attention to names of articles, specifications, quantities, prices and units.

Completeness

Completeness means that business letters should contain all the necessary information. When writing a letter, all the matters should be discussed in a replying letter, and all the questions should be answered. Only a complete letter can work efficiently. Check your letters before sending them.

Conciseness

Conciseness means complete information by using brief expressions. A good and effective business letter should be clear, concise and without any repetition. To achieve this, try to avoid using stale and roundabout phrases. The elimination of wordy business jargon can also help to make a letter clearer and at the same time more concise. Furthermore, organize each paragraph carefully and make sure a point to each paragraph.

Clarity/Clearness

A good business letter should avoid being misunderstood. An ambiguous letter will not only cause trouble but also waste time of both sides. Make all the necessary points clear, full, and in a logical sequence. Good, straightforward and simple English is preferable in business letter writing.

Keep the purpose of this letter in mind, use proper words and phrases in correct sentence structure, and then you can write a clear letter.

Courtesy

Courtesy means showing consideration for your correspondent and respect for your readers' feelings. You need to prepare every message with the readers in mind and try to put yourself in their shoes. It allows a refusal to business without killing hopes of future business. There are some tips for being courtesy: reply promptly to your customer; understand and respect the recipient's point of view; be tactful and try not to cause offence if you feel some comments are unfair.

2. Basic Parts of Business English Letters

A business letter usually consists of the following 13 parts.

An ordinary business letter consists of 7 essential parts:

(1) Letterhead

(2) Reference and Date

(3) Inside Name and Address

(4) Salutation

(5) Body of the Letter

(6) Complimentary Close

(7) Signature

Besides, there are 6 optional parts:

(8) Attention Line

(9) Subject Line

(10) Reference Notation

(11) Enclosure Notation

(12) Carbon Copy Notation

(13) Postscript

Basic Knowledge of Business English Letters Writing

BEIJING ITT HARDWARE PRODUCTS IMP.&EXP. CORP.
82 DONGANMEN STREET
Email: davy_qi@ itthw.inf.com
Fax: 86-10-62536891

Letterhead

Our ref: 011/te
Your ref: NT/kb
Date: April 25, 2019

Reference and Date

Compaq Computers
20555 SH 249, Houston TX77070
USA

Inside Name and Address

Attention: Import Department

Attention Line

Dear Sirs,

Salutation

Re: Key Boards

Subject Line

Thanks for your letter of April 22nd.

Body of the Letter

As requested, we are sending you herewith a copy of our latest price list for your reference.

Please note that all prices are understood to be subject to our final confirmation.

We look forward to receiving your kind comments.

Yours faithfully,

Complimentary Close

Beijing ITT hardware products Imp. & Exp. corp.
(Sig) __Harry Wang__
       Manager

Signature

HW/yl

Reference Notation

Encl: as stated

Enclosure Notation

cc: our branch office

Carbon Copy Notation

P.S. Your letter of the April 24th has just arrived. We will look into the matter and reply to you soon.

Postscript

(1) Letterhead

The letterhead includes the essential particulars about the writer—name, address, telephone number, fax number and email address of the company. It is printed at the top of the paper, helping to form the recipient's impression of the writer's firm. A neat, well-balanced letterhead is preferable to enhance the prestige of the firm that uses it.

(2) Reference and Date

The reference number is used for filing and consulting. It is always at the left margin below the letterhead. It may include a file number, a contract number or the initials of the signer and typist. They are marked with "Our ref." and "Your ref".

The date should be put below the reference number at right margin for indented form or at the left margin for full block form. Type the date all in one line. Do not use figures or abbreviations for the month, or it will cause confusion.

Examples：

6th July, 2019(British English)

6 July, 2019(British English)

July 6th, 2019(American English)

July 6, 2019(American English)

(3) Inside Name and Address

The inside name and address is the name and address of the recipient, which should be exactly the same as what appears on the envelope. There are three advantages of inside name and address. Firstly, the inside name and address can make sure the letter will be put into the right envelope. Secondly, it is easy for consulting and filing. Thirdly, it is convenient for envelope with transparent window.

Example：

Mr. Thomas R Witter, Manager

Providence Insurance Company Inc.

892 Market Street

Chicago, IL 60601

USA

(4) **Salutation**

Salutation is a polite way to greet the addressee. It is typed at the left margin below the inside name and address.

The particular form used of salutation depends upon the writer's relationship with his recipient and it must agree with the form of complimentary close.

Remember that the salutation always appears on a line by itself and is followed by a comma or a colon.

Examples:

Dear Mr. / Ms. Green,

Dear Madam or Sir,

Dear Mesdames or Sirs,

(5) **Body of the Letter**

It is the most important part of business letter since the main purpose of the letter is to convey a message. To make this part effective, you must adhere to 5C Principles and carefully paragraph.

① Write simply, clearly, grammatically and to the point.

② Paragraph carefully, confining each paragraph to one topic. Generally speaking, the letter is divided into three parts: opening, actual message and closing.

③ Use margins tactfully and keep the letter in an attractive display.

(6) **Complimentary Close**

The complimentary close, like the salutation, is a polite way of ending a letter.

It is below the body of the letter at the left margin or the right margin according to different forms of layout.

The complimentary close should agree with the salutation; in other words, the expression of salutation settles the form of complimentary close.

Salutation	Close	Occasion
Dear Sirs/ Mesdames/ Sir/ Madam,	Yours faithfully,	formal, British English
Dear Mr. / Ms. Green,	Yours sincerely,	less formal, common in modern business
Gentlemen:	Yours truly,	formal, American English

(7) Signature

The signature is the signed name or mark of the person writing the letter or that of the firm he represents. It should be written in ink. As many hand-written signatures are illegible, typed signatures are necessarily followed by the title or position.

Note: Your written signature should stick to one style.

The signatures written and typed must correspond exactly.

Example:

The overseas Co., Ltd

(signature)

John Smith

General Manager, Sales Department

(8) Attention Line

The attention line is useful when the letter is addressed direct to a particular person or a department of a firm. In some cases, it is considered a part of the inside name and address. It is usually typed two lines above the salutation, as shown below:

Theo Tureon Equipment Inc.

575 Rue Marais Vanier

Quebec, Canada

For the attention of Import Department

or

Attention: Bill Smith

(9) Subject Line

Subject line, like a title of the letter, indicates at a glance the general content or purpose of the letter. Generally it is followed by "Re:" or "Subject:" and underlined or capitalized.

Examples:

Re: Contract No. 123

Subject: Contract No. 123

Contract No. 123

(10) Reference Notation

The reference notation consists of the initials of the writer and the typist, which are separated by a colon or a stroke. They are placed two line spaces below the signature against the left margin. If the name of the writer is typed in the signature area, it only shows the initials of the typist.

Examples:

ms

JB / ms

JB: ms

(11) Enclosure Notation

Enclosure notation shows that there are some documents to be sent with the letter, such as catalogues, price lists, invoices, copies of faxes or order sheets, etc.

The enclosure notation is usually placed two lines below the signature or the reference notation. It can be marked by the following way:

Enclosure

Encls. 5

Encls. 2 catalogues

      1 price list

Enc. as stated

(12) Carbon Copy Notation

Carbon copy notation shows that there are copies of the letter sent to others. There are two kinds of carbon copy notation, cc or bcc. The former one means recipient knows that copies are sent while the latter one means the recipient know nothing about the copies.

(13) Postscript

In a business letter, postscript, or its abbreviation P.S. is used for emphasis and attracting the readers' attention.

Try to avoid P.S. as a way of adding important points. Rewrite the body of the letter if you forgot to mention something important.

3. Basic Layouts of Business English Letters

The layout of format is the visual organization of a business letter and it makes the first and important impression on the reader. Although choice of layout is a matter of personal taste, it is safe to follow one form of layout and stick to it so as to avoid confusion and waste of time for business letters. There are three common layouts of business letters:

(1) Indented Style

(2) Full-block Style

(3) Modified Block Style

(1) Indented Style 缩进式

This is a traditional British style. The attention line and subject line should be centered, and the first lines of each paragraph in the body should be all indented 3 to 8 spaces to show the separation of paragraph clearly. The date, complimentary close and signature should be placed at the right margin.

Overseas Trading Co.

21 Park Street, London EC4, England

Phone: 360-555-1212

Fax: 360-555-1515

Tobalcom@yahoo.com

Our Reference No. J/W-CO18
Your Reference No.

January 5th, 2019

Anhui Foreign Trading Corp.
31 Changjiang Road
Hefei, Anhui Province
China

Attention: Import Department

Dear Mr. Zhang,

Re: Catalogue & Pricelist

  Thank you for your letter of January 2nd. We shall be glad to enter into business relations with your company. In compliance with your request, we are sending you, under separate cover, our latest catalogue and pricelist covering our export range.

  We are looking forward to your first enquiry.

Yours sincerely,

Overseas Trading Co.

John Smith

John Smith

Basic Knowledge of Business English Letters Writing

(2) Full-block Style 完全齐头式

The full-block style is more popular in modern business. The feature of this style is that all the parts should be flush with the left margin except the letterhead.

Overseas Trading Co.
21 Park Street, London EC4, England
Phone: 360-555-1212
Fax: 360-555-1515
Tobalcom@yahoo.com

Our Reference No. J/W-CO18
Your Reference No.

January 5th, 2019

Anhui Foreign Trading Corp.
31 Changjiang Road
Hefei, Anhui Province
China

Attention: Import Department

Dear Mr. Zhang,

Re: Catalogue & Price list

Thank you for your letter of January 2nd. We shall be glad to enter into business relations with your company. In compliance with your request, we are sending you, under separate cover, our latest catalogue and price list covering our export range.

We are looking forward to your first enquiry.

Yours sincerely,

Overseas Trading Co.
John Smith
John Smith

13

(3) Modified Block Style 改良齐头式

To avoid the disadvantages of full-block style, some writers prefer to put the date, complimentary close and signature at the right margin for better filing and consulting. This style combined advantages of indented style and full-block style.

Overseas Trading Co.
21 Park Street, London EC4, England
Phone: 360-555-1212
Fax: 360-555-1515
Tobalcom@yahoo.com

Our Reference No. J/W-CO18
Your Reference No.

January 5th, 2019

Anhui Foreign Trading Corp.
31 Changjiang Road
Hefei, Anhui Province
China

Attention: Import Department

Dear Mr. Zhang,

Re: Catalogue & Price list

Thank you for your letter of January 2nd. We shall be glad to enter into business relations with your company. In compliance with your request, we are sending you, under separate cover, our latest catalogue and price list covering our export range.

We are looking forward to your first enquiry.

Yours sincerely,

Overseas Trading Co.

John Smith

John Smith

4. Emails

Electronic mail (email) is a method of exchanging messages ("mail") between people using electronic devices. Invented by Ray Tomlinson, email first entered limited use in the 1960s and by the mid-1970s had taken the form as now recognized. Email operates across computer networks, which today is primarily the Internet.

Email servers accept, forward, deliver and store messages.

Structures of email are similar to those of correspondence. Email generally contains the following parts:

From/Sender: the email address, and optionally the name of the author(s). If you want to give the receiver a clear appearance, you can set up with the name of your company.

Date: the local time and date when the message was written. This is also filled in automatically by the computer.

To: the email address(es), and optionally name(s) of the message's recipient(s). Indicates primary recipients (multiple allowed), for secondary recipients see "Cc" and "Bcc" below.

Subject: a brief summary of the topic of the message. Certain abbreviations are commonly used in the subject, including "RE" and "FW". A perfect subject will attract the recipient to read your email, especially for the first email to a potential client. When draft the subject, you can use some abbreviations or tips in this line, such as RE, meaning that you are responding to the question; URGENT, meaning that this message is time critical; FYI, meaning that for your information only and no reply is required; REQ, meaning actions required.

Cc: carbon copy. If you want to send the email to other person besides the recipient, you can use the CC., just filling the email address of the person.

Bcc: blind carbon copy. Addresses are usually only specified during SMTP delivery, and not usually listed in the message header. In this way, you can prevent giving out someone's address. For example, when you send an email message to 10 people and use "To" or "CC", all 10 people can see each other's email address. However, by using "BCC" each receiver see only two-theirs and yours.

Body: the message itself and quite similar to the forms of a letter. It contains salutation, the actual message and the complimentary close.

Signature: referring to the signature of your email in business. You'd better give enough information about your business, including your name, contact details and the information of your company. Setting up the signature in advance helps you to use the set signature without writing it every time.

Enclosure: If you want to send any pictures, documents or other information such as catalogues, price lists or copies of shipping documents, you can attach them with the email by enclosure.

Example:

To	Flora White
From	Jane Li
Subject	Quotation Sheet
Enclosure	quotation

Dear Flora,

Thanks for mailing me back and notifying us your requested item with details!

Please find the detailed price list in attachment. Samples could be prepared on request.

Please contact us if you have any other questions.

Sincerely yours,

Jane Li

Part IV Practical Training

1. Choose the best answer.

(1) To avoid any ambiguity or misunderstanding, the business letter should adhere to the principle of ____.

    A. completeness   B. clearness   C. courtesy   D. conciseness

(2) ____ is an important feature of business letters by using a friendly tone and wording of good feelings.

    A. Completeness   B. Clearness   C. Courtesy   D. Conciseness

(3) For a normal business letter format, some people prefer to use "Regards" or

"Yours sincerely". This part is called ____.

    A. complimentary close   B. signature

    C. letterhead   D. the body of the letter

(4) The mainly used style is ____. In this style, all the parts except letterhead are typed from the left margin.

    A. the indented style   B. the full-block style

    C. the modified block style   D. the half block style

(5) People receive a huge number of emails which are present in the mailboxes every day. To get your email noticed among them, it is important to give your email a ____ that grabs the attention of the receiver.

    A. letterhead   B. subject line   C. message   D. closing part

2. Writing.

Practice the usage of emails. Try to get familiar with the function of emails by sending emails to your teacher or classmates.

Module 2
Business Negotiation
业务磋商

Unit 2　Establishing Business Relations
建立业务关系

Lead-in

Try to finish the following tasks and find out the learning objectives of this unit.

Task 1

　　假设你是广州轻工业产品进出口公司的外贸业务员，希望与英国一家公司建立业务往来，因此代表公司致函对方。内容如下：

敬启者：

　　我方从我国驻英国大使馆的商务参赞处获悉贵公司的名称和地址。现写此信，希望在平等互利、互通有无的基础上与贵方建立业务关系。

　　我方与我们当地各大工业品经销商关系密切，如贵方报价具有竞争性，我方定能大量销售贵方产品。

　　惠请贵公司告知你方出售货物的详情和价格，如可能，请附样品。我方乐意研究贵方产品在我方市场销售的可能性。

Task 2

　　假设你是杭州纺织品进出口公司的外贸业务员，希望与美国一家贸易公司建立贸易关系，因此代表公司致函对方。内容如下：

敬启者：

　　经 ABC 公司介绍，我们很荣幸得知贵公司的名称和地址。我公司专营中国纺织品出口业务，希望在平等互利的基础上与贵方建立直接的业务关系。

　　为让贵方了解我方产品，特邮寄去我们最新的目录及价目表，供贵方参考。如果贵方对目录中所列商品感兴趣，请具体询盘。

　　期待贵方早日回复。

Part Ⅰ　Introduction

没有顾客就没有市场,没有市场就谈不上贸易。为了开拓市场、经营产品、维系和拓展业务,建立业务关系便成为了对外贸易的第一步。需要通过各种途径对潜在客户的相关信息及需求进行全面了解并进行沟通。

建立外贸业务关系的函电要写得诚恳、真挚、礼貌,这种函电的结构一般包括四个方面:

(1) 说明信息来源,告知对方你从何渠道得知对方的姓名和地址。获得客户信息的途径如下:参加交易会或博览会、国内外的商会、商务参赞处或其他商务组织、贸易伙伴的介绍、代表团互访、银行牵线、广告等;

(2) 对公司作简单的介绍,例如公司的业务范围,稍稍宣传一下产品和服务;

(3) 写信的目的。你想与对方做什么生意,比如,想购买对方的产品、推荐自己的产品、想与对方建立合资公司等;

(4) 表达想与对方合作和早日收到回复的愿望。

无论是买方还是卖方,收到建立业务关系请求的函电后,都应该迅速、完整、礼貌地作出答复,以便给对方留下良好的印象。一般回复建立业务关系的函电包括如下方面:

(1) 感谢对方对本公司感兴趣;

(2) 表示对对方建立业务关系意愿的兴趣;

(3) 表述进一步采取的行动。

Part Ⅱ　Letter Writing Guide

Having obtained the desired names and address, you can write "First Letter" or circulars to the party concerned. Generally speaking, the type of letter should begin by telling the receiver how his name is known. Then some general information should be given as to:

(1) The source from which you get the information. (How and where you get the name and address of receiver's company.)

(2) Your intention or desire of writing the letter. (State your purpose in writing—your wish to build up business relations with the firm in question.)

(3) The business scope of your company. (Briefly introduce your business and main scope of products.)

(4) The reference as to your company's financial status and integrity. (Offer credit references if possible.)

If you intend to purchase something, you may also request for samples, catalogs, price lists, etc. And you should state simply, clearly, concisely and politely what you can sell and what you expect to buy. And at the end of the letter, you should express your expectation of cooperation and an early reply.

The first impression matters very much. Be positive to follow the standard format and try best to avoid making mistakes.

Upon receipt of any letter of this nature, be sure to answer in full without the least delay and with courtesy so as to create goodwill and leave a good impression on the sender.

When replying, you should:

(1) Express thanks to the sender for the proposal.

(2) Provide information requested.

(3) State clearly if you accept the proposal or not.

Give a reason if you decline it, and end your letter with a positive tone for future business.

Part Ⅲ Sample Letters

1. Self-introduction

Dear Sirs,

Thank you for your interest in our company. Medi Health Co., Ltd. is one of the largest exporters of medical and surgical instruments in Singapore. We have over 30 years of experience in this line and have been at the cutting edge of new technology innovations due to our sophisticated recruitment of the best creative group of talent researchers from both China and abroad.

Enclosed please find a copy of our updated brochure detailing our company's history, its pioneering achievements in this field and its full range of products we are handling.

Again, we appreciate your interest in our business very much. If you have any further questions, please feel free to contact us.

Sincerely yours,

Medi Health Co., Ltd

×××

 Notes

1. Co., Ltd. 有限公司

    英语中表示公司的词很多,常用的有 company, corporation, firm, house 等。Co., Ltd. 是 Company Limited 的缩写,表示责任有限公司。Corp. Inc. 是 Corporation incorporated 的缩写,表示股份有限公司。

2. line [lain] n.（商务英语中）行业,业务;货品种类,系列

    e.g. We are introducing ourselves as one of the leading exporters of the same line of business.

    我公司是一家同行业的领导性出口企业。

    e.g. They recommended a fashion line in hats that suit the European market.

    他们推荐了一款适合欧洲市场的时尚的帽子。

3. innovation [ˌinəˈveiʃn] n. 创造,创新;改革

    e.g. We must promote originality and encourage innovation.

    我们必须提倡原创,鼓励革新。

4. due to 由于

    该词是外贸函电常用语,也可用 owing to/on account of/because of/as a result of/thanks to 等。要注意,这些都是介词短语,其后只能接名词。而 because/since/as/for（因为）等是连词,其后接句子。

5. sophisticated [səˈfistikeitid] adj. 见多识广的；老练的；先进的；精密的；在行的

    e.g. You must understand you are dealing with an extremely sophisticated audience.

    你必须明白你面对的是一群经验丰富的听众。

6. recruitment [riˈkruːtmənt] n. 招收;招募,招聘

    e.g. Provide necessary recruitment strategies for marketing and sales support control.

    为市场营销支持控制提供必要的招聘战略。

7. enclosed [inˈkləʊzd] adj. 随函附上的

    e.g. Enclosed please find our price list.

    随函寄去我方价目单一份,请查收。

8. appreciate [əˈpriːʃieit] v. 感谢,感激

    该词在函电中的使用频率远远超过 thank,用法也不同。其宾语只能是 sth. 而不能是 sb.。

    e.g. We highly appreciate your long cooperation.

    非常感谢贵方的长期合作。

e.g. We'll appreciate it if you would send us your catalog soon.

如尽快寄来商品目录,我方不胜感激。

2. A Request for the Establishment of Business Relations

Dear Sirs,

Your letter of November 21st addressed to our Embassy in Bangkok has been transferred to us for attention.

As the items mentioned in it fall within the scope of our business activities, we shall be pleased to enter into direct business relations with you. We have learned that you are one of the leading importers and wholesalers of Electric and Electronic Machinery and Equipment in Thailand. We are exporters of the same lines of business, having a business background of some 40 years, and are now particularly interested in exporting to your country Electronic Products of all types.

All kinds of our products are good sellers and worth commendation for their excellent quality. If you are interested in marketing these products at your end, please let us know and we shall be pleased to send you our quotations and sample books upon receipt of your specific enquiries.

Looking forward to your favorable reply.

Yours faithfully,

×××

 Notes

1. embassy ['embəsi] *n.* 大使馆;(统称)使馆官员

    e.g. The embassy says it has telexed their demands to the foreign ministry.

    大使馆表示已通过电传将他们的要求发送给外交部了。

2. transfer ['trænsfɜ:(r)] *n.* 搬迁;转移;调动;(旅途中的)中转,换乘,改变路线

    [træns'fɜ:(r)] *v.* (使)转移,搬迁;(使)调动;转职;让与,转让(权力等)

    e.g. How can I transfer money from my bank account to his?

    怎么才能把我账户上的钱转到他的账户上呢?

3. attention [ə'tenʃn] *n.* 注意;专心;留心

在外贸函电中常译为"办理,处理"。

e.g. Your enquiry of May 8th for shoes and gloves has been passed on to us for our attention.

你方5月8日关于鞋和手套的询盘已转交我方处理。

4. business ['bɪznəs] n. 交易,买卖(不可数名词);工商企业,公司(可数名词)

e.g. We have concluded substantial business with that company.

我们已与该公司达成大量交易。

e.g. There are many businesses engaged in that trade.

众多公司从事那项贸易。

5. particularly [pə'tɪkjələli] adv. 特别地;尤其(= especially)

e.g. The last thing we want to do is to disappoint a customer, particularly an old customer like you.

我们最不愿让顾客失望,特别是像您这样的老顾客。

6. commendation [ˌkɒmen'deɪʃn] n. 赞扬;赞成;推荐

e.g. He was very proud when his daughter received a commendation for her achievement.

他女儿因成绩优异而受到嘉奖,他为此感到很自豪。

7. specific [spə'sɪfɪk] adj. 明确的;具体的;特定的;特有的;独特的

e.g. We have set specific objectives and deadlines to continually improve performance.

我们设立了具体的目标和完成期限以持续不断地改善业绩。

3. Making Credit Investigation

Gentlemen:

We are Export Department of China National Import & Export Corporation. From a financial report we know you have business contact with the under-mentioned firm, of Accra, Ghana.

The firm has lately approached us, asking to establish business relations with us and promote the sales of our chemical products in the Republic of Ghana as our sub-agents:
West African Import/Export Co.
16.O. Box 242, Accra
GHANA

We would therefore highly appreciate it if you would let us have information about the financial and business standing of the above firm.

Any information that you may give would be treated in strict confidence and would doubtless be very much appreciated.

Yours faithfully,

×××

 Notes

1. approach [əˈprəʊtʃ] n. 方式,方法;态度　v. 靠近,接近;接洽;建议;要求
   表示与……联系,此时是及物动词,不能再与介词 with 搭配,contact 也是如此。
   e.g. As soon as any fresh supply comes in, we'll approach (不可再用 with) you.
   一旦有新货源,我们会与你联系。

2. agent [ˈeidʒənt] n. (企业、政治等的)代理人,经纪人
   e.g. We are not prepared to point a sole agent in your district.
   我们不准备在贵地区指定独家代理商。

3. financial [faiˈnænʃl] adj. 财政的;财务的;金融的;有钱的
   e.g. I admit we are under some time pressure as well as financial pressure.
   我承认我们现在也面临着一些时间和财务上的压力。

4. standing [ˈstændiŋ] n. 名声;地位;级别;身份
   business standing 营业状况;商业信用状况
   e.g. After paying due consideration to your proposals and investigating your business standing, we have decided to appoint you as our agent in the district.
   在适当考虑了你方建议和调查你方营业状况之后,我们已经决定指定你方为这一地区的业务代理。

5. confidence [ˈkɒnfidəns] n. 信心;信任,信赖;秘密,机密
   in confidence 保密
   e.g. As for anything told to me in confidence, my lips are sealed.
   至于私下告知我的任何事情,我都会守口如瓶。

6. doubtless [ˈdaʊtləs] adv. 大概;几乎肯定地
   e.g. This is doubtless quite true.
   这无疑是千真万确的。

4. Favorable and Unfavorable Reply to Credit Investigation

（1）**Favorable Reply**

Dear Sirs,

We are pleased to send you, in confidence, the credit information you requested concerning ABC Engineering Company of New Zealand in your letter of May 12th, 2019. The above firm enjoys the fullest respect and unquestionable confidence in the business world. They are prompt and punctual in all their transactions, and we have no hesitation in giving them credit to an amount considerably beyond the sum you mentioned. However, this is without obligation on our part. We hope this information may be of use to you.

Yours faithfully,

×××

（2）**Unfavorable Reply**

Dear Sirs,

We have received your letter of May 12th, 2019, respecting the standing of ABC Engineering Company of New Zealand.

We regret to say that we have to make in reply an unfavorable communication to you. The mentioned firm is known to be heavily committed and have overrun their reserves. They are being pressed by several creditors and their position is precarious. Caution is advisable.

Please consider this information as given in strict confidence.

Yours faithfully,

×××

 Notes

1. transaction [trænˈzækʃn] *n.* 交易，业务，买卖（可数名词）；办理，处理

    e.g. They have made huge profit out of the transaction.

    他们从这笔交易中获得了巨额利润。

2. considerably [kən'sidərəbli] adv. 非常；很；相当多地

   e.g. The economic situation has changed considerably.

   经济形势已发生了相当大的变化。

3. obligation [ˌɒbli'geiʃn] n. 义务；职责,责任

   e.g. They reminded him of his contractual obligations.

   他们提醒他注意合同规定的义务。

4. respecting [ri'spektiŋ] prep. 关于(= concerning)

   e.g. We confirm our call of last week respecting our offers to you.

   关于上周本公司通过电话给您的报价,我们特予以确认。

5. overrun ['əuvərʌn] n. 泛滥成灾；超过限度 [ˌəuvə'rʌn] v. 泛滥；横行；肆虐；多用(时间、钱财等)；超时

   e.g. You've overrun your time by 10 minutes.

   你超时10分钟了。

6. creditors ['kreditə(r)] n. 债权人,债主；贷方

   e.g. The company said it would pay in full all its creditors.

   该公司称将偿清所有债权人的债务。

7. precarious [pri'keəriəs] adj. 不稳的；不确定的；不保险的；危险的

   e.g. Our financial situation had become precarious.

   我们的财务状况已变得不稳定。

Part Ⅳ Useful Expressions and Sentences

Expressions

1. in this line 在这个行业
2. at the cutting edge of 在……前沿,处于……的领先地位
3. due to 由于
4. both China and abroad 国内外
5. Enclosed please find 随函请查收
6. transfer to 转到
7. for attention 以供办理
8. fall within the scope of one's business activities 属于……的经营范围
9. enter into direct business relations with you 与贵方建立业务关系
10. establish business(trade) relations(relationship) with ... 与……建立业务关系
11. worth commendation 值得称赞

12. at your end = in your district/ area/ place/ territory 在你地,在你处
13. upon receipt of 一收到……就……
14. look forward to 期盼
15. promote the sales of 促销
16. We would highly appreciate it if 如能……不胜感激
17. be of use 有用处,起作用
18. in strict confidence 严格保密
19. on one's part = on the part of 在……方面
20. be heavily committed = to have heavy commitments 承诺过多,接受订单过多

Typical Sentences

1. We have over 30 years of experience in this line and have been at the cutting edge of new technology innovations due to our sophisticated recruitment of the best creative group of talent researchers from both China and abroad.

2. Enclosed please find a copy of our updated brochure detailing our company's history, its pioneering achievements in this field and its full range of products we are handling.

3. If you have any further questions, please feel free to contact us.

4. As the items mentioned in it fall within the scope of our business activities, we shall be pleased to enter into direct business relations with you.

5. If you are interested in marketing these products at your end, please let us know and we shall be pleased to send you our quotations and sample books upon receipt of your specific enquiries.

6. We would therefore highly appreciate it if you would let us have information about the financial and business standing of the above firm.

7. We hope this information may be of use to you.

8. We regret to say that we have to make in reply an unfavorable communication to you.

9. The mentioned firm is known to be heavily committed and have overrun their reserves.

10. Please consider this information as given in strict confidence.

Part Ⅴ　Practical Training

Ⅰ. Elementary Training

1. Choose the best answer.

(1) We are a state-operated corporation ____ both the import and export of textiles.
   A. handling in   B. trading   C. dealing with   D. dealing in

(2) We have the goods you asked for in stock and will deliver as soon as we ____ your order.
   A. receive   B. received   C. receiving   D. will receive

(3) We have pleasure in enclosing a copy of our latest catalogue ____ for in your letter dated December 11th.
   A. ask   B. asks   C. asked   D. asking

(4) We ____ herewith two copies of our illustrated catalogue for your consideration.
   A. include   B. enclose   C. inquire   D. exclude

(5) Our products are of better quality than ____ from other countries.
   A. that   B. those   C. this   D. it

(6) We owe your name and address ____ the Commercial Counselor's Office of the Swedish Embassy in Beijing.
   A. to   B. for   C. with   D. by

(7) Ours is a ____ corporation.
   A. state operated   B. state-operated
   C. state operation   D. state-operating

(8) We are very pleased ____ business relations with your firm.
   A. entering into   B. to enter   C. to enter into   D. entering

(9) We shall ____ a reply soon.
   A. appreciate your giving   B. appreciate you to give
   C. appreciate you for giving   D. appreciate for your giving

(10) By joint efforts we can ____ both friendship and business.
   A. increase   B. expand   C. speed up   D. promote

2. Read the following letters and fill in each blank with prepositions.

Letter 1

Dear Sirs,

We know (1) your information posted on *Alibaba.com* that you are (2) the market (3) textiles. We would like to take this opportunity to introduce our company and products, (4) the hope that we may work (5) Beijing Textiles Import & Export Corporation (6) the future.

We are a joint venture specializing in the manufacture and export (7) textiles. We have enclosed our catalogue, which introduces our company (8) detail and covers the main products we supply at present. You may also visit our online company introduction which includes our latest product line.

Should any of these items be (9) interest to you, please let us know. We will be happy to give you a quotation upon receipt of your detailed requirements.

We look forward (10) receiving your inquiries soon.

Yours truly,

×××

Letter 2

Dear Sirs,

Your communication (1) May 28th addressed to our sister corporation in Shanghai has been passed (2) to us (3) attention and reply as the export of enamelware falls (4) the scope of our business activities.

However, we very much regret that we are not (5) a position to supply you with enamelware directly, as we are already represented by Messrs. Freemen and Brothers Co., Ltd., 267 Broad Street for the sales of this commodity (6) your district. We would advise you to get in touch (7) them (8) your requirements.

In case you are interested in other items, kindly let us know and we shall be pleased to make you offers directly.

Yours faithfully,

×××

 3. Translate the following English into Chinese.

(1) wide in range

(2) fall within the scope of

(3) in the market for

(4) at your end

(5) for your reference

(6) expand trade

(7) in the line of

(8) specialize in

(9) acquaint you with

(10) be heavily committed

(11) Your company has been kindly recommended to us by the Chamber of Commerce in London, Britain as one of the leading exporters of cotton textiles in your country.

(12) We wish to inform you that we specialize in the export of Chinese textiles and shall be glad to enter into business relations with you on the basis of equality and mutual benefit.

(13) The Bank of China has recommended your company as being interested in establishing business relations with a Chinese company for the purpose of exporting various products of your country and importing Chinese manufactured goods.

(14) We've come to know your name and address from the Commercial Counselor's Office of the Chinese Embassy in London.

(15) We'd like to express our desire to establish business relations with you on the basis of equality, mutual benefit and the exchange of needed goods.

(16) Our purpose is to explore the possibilities of developing trade with you.

(17) We are a state-owned company specializing in the export of table-cloth.

(18) We are the largest food trading company in Japan, and have offices or representatives in all major cities in Japan.

(19) As the items fall within the scope of our business activities, we shall be pleased

to enter into direct business relations with you.

(20) In order to acquaint you with the textiles we handle, we take pleasure in sending you by air our latest catalogue for your perusal.

II. Intermediate Training

1. Supply the missing words in the blanks of the following letter. The first letters are given.

Dear Sirs,

We o____ your name and address f____ the Commercial Counselor's Office of Chinese Embassy in the UK. We take this opportunity to write to you with a view to s____ up business relations with you.

We are a state-owned company dealing specially i____ the export of tablecloth. We are in a p____ to accept orders according t____ the customer's samples.

In order to give you a g____ idea of various kinds of the tablecloth we are h____, we are airmailing you by separate c____ our latest catalogue for your reference. Please let us know immediately if you are interested in our products. We will send our price list and s____ to you as soon as we receive your specific inquiry.

We look forward to your early reply.

Yours faithfully,

× × ×

2. Cloze. Choose the most suitable words from the list of words to fill in the blanks. Each word can be used only once.

form   exchange   invisible   attractive   necessities
reproduction   sufficiency   transportation   division   meet

International trade is the ___(1)___ of goods and services produced in one country for goods and services produced in another country. In addition to visible trade, which involves the import and export of goods and merchandise, there is also ___(2)___ trade, which involves the exchange of services between nations. Nations such as Greece and Norway have large maritime fleets which could provide ___(3)___ services. This is a kind of invisible trade. Invisible trade can be as important to some nations as the export of raw materials or commodities to others. In both cases, the nations earn the money to buy ___(4)___.

There is no country in the world that can produce all the products it needs. Thus countries join in the international ___(5)___ of labor for effective production and ___(6)___. Sometimes a country can buy goods and services from abroad on a barter（易货）basis. Barter means doing business by exchanging goods of one sort for goods of another sort without using money. Barter trade itself is not enough to ___(7)___ a country's import needs. But as a ___(8)___ of international trade, it is still ___(9)___ in developing countries where foreign exchange is in short supply and the inflow of foreign funds is far from ___(10)___ to meet their obligations in the external trade.

3. Translate the following Chinese into English.

(1) 业务关系

(2) 平等互利

(3) 转交

(4) 有限公司

(5) 供你方参考

(6) 专营

(7) 主要出口商

(8) 促进贸易

(9) 一系列

(10) 具体询盘

(11) 我公司作为纺织品出口商已有多年。我们的产品质量好、价格合理，在世界上享有极高的声誉。

(12) 我公司是中国最大的电器用品进口商。

(13) 我们十分愿意与贵公司建立直接的贸易关系。

(14) 如果你方对我们的产品有兴趣，请尽快通知我方。一旦收到你方具体询盘，即寄送报价单和样品。

(15) 很高兴能有机会恢复我们的友好关系。

(16) 我们写此信的目的是与你方建立业务关系。

(17) 请向我们推荐一些最可靠的中国手工艺品的出口商，可以吗？

(18) 我们将尽力扩大同你们的贸易关系。

(19) 我们公司主要经营手工艺品。

(20) 我们一直对在中国投资很感兴趣。

Ⅲ. Advanced Training

 1. Translate the following letter into English.

敬启者：

  贵方7月5日电动机的询盘收悉，因该商品属中国国家进出口公司的经营范围，我方已将贵方询盘转交他们办理，请直接就贵方所需与他们联系。

  借此机会向贵方介绍，我方是经营中国工艺品出口业务的一家国有企业，与世界各地的大商号都建立了广泛的联系。

  随函附上我方的最新目录和价目单，请查收。希望能和贵方建立业务关系。

 2. Write a letter in English.

  You are asked to write a letter or send an email to a foreign company for establishing business relations. The letter or the email should cover at least the following points：

  (1) Where have you got the information?

  (2) What is your desire?

  (3) What is your business scope?

  (4) How about your financial standing?

Unit 3 Inquiry and Offer
询盘与发盘

Lead-in

Try to finish the following tasks and find out the learning objectives of this unit.

Task 1

假设你是中国一进口公司的外贸业务员,最近你公司打算从英国一公司进口 100 台真空吸尘器(vacuum cleaner)。现在,请致函该公司向其询盘,注意信中务必包含以下内容:
(1) 我们在广交会(Canton Fair)上得知贵公司以及贵公司的产品。
(2) 我方是中国上海主要的吸尘器经销商。
(3) 我方拟购 100 台 V368 号真空吸尘器,如能详报含 2%佣金的成本保险加运费至上海的最低价,将不胜感激。
(4) 报盘时,请说明支付条款、最早装运期、包装条款以及折扣等方面的情况。
(5) 盼立即回复。

Task 2

假设你是中国一进出口公司的外贸业务员,最近你公司收到德国一公司的询盘信。现在,请代表公司就你们的男士休闲鞋向其发实盘。注意信中务必包含以下内容:
(1) 贵公司 2018 年 3 月 4 日发来的询盘信已经收悉,谢谢你方对我们的产品感兴趣。
(2) 应贵公司要求,特向贵方报实盘如下:
品名:远足牌男士休闲鞋(Hiking Brand Men's Casual Shoes)
规格:棕色橡胶底(Rubber Soles),黑色棉布鞋面(Cotton Uppers)
尺寸:大码 50%,中码 50%(large 50%, medium 50%)
包装:每件塑料袋内装一双男士休闲鞋,每一加固纸板箱(enforced carton)内装 2 打
数量:200 打

价格:每打100美元,成本保险加运费至汉堡
交货:2018年7月15日之前
支付:在保兑的不可撤销的信用证条件下凭即期汇票支付
(3) 此盘为实盘,北京时间2018年3月15日下午5点前收到贵方回复为有效。
(4) 我们相信这些产品会满足贵方的要求,盼尽早收到订单。

Part Ⅰ　Introduction

询盘,又称为询价,通常由买方作出,询问一些有关预定货物的细节问题,如价格、目录、交货日期及其他条款。

询盘可以分为两种,一种只询问价格,索取商品目录或样品,被称为一般询盘;另一种询盘则包含特定商品的各种交易条件,被称为具体询盘。

一般询盘并不一定立即接触具体交易,大多具摸底性质。其内容包括:要求寄某种商品的样品、目录和价目表;探寻某种商品的品质、数量、价格、交货期等。

具体询盘实际上就是请求对方报盘,即当买方已准备购买某种商品时,请卖主就这一商品报价。

发盘,也叫报盘、报价,是外贸业务流程的一个重要组成部分。发盘是交易的一方(发盘人)向另一方(受盘人)提出购买或出售某种商品的各项条件(包括数量、价格、交货期、付款条件等),并愿意按照这些条件与对方达成交易并订立合同。在发盘有效期内,发盘人不得任意撤销或修改其内容,一经对方接受,将受其约束,并承担按照发盘条件与对方订立合同的法律责任。发盘的交易条件可以采用分条列项的形式醒目清楚地写出。

发盘应包括哪些内容呢?关于这一点,各国的法律规定不尽相同。有些国家法律要求对合同的主要条件,如品名、品质、数量、包装、价格、交货时间与地点以及支付办法等,都要有完整、明确、肯定的规定,并不得附有任何保留条件,以便受盘人一旦接受即可签订一项对买卖双方都有约束力的合同。而《联合国国际货物销售合同公约》(以下简称《公约》)规定发盘至少包括三个基本要素:(1)标明货物的名称;(2)明示或默示地规定货物的数量或规定数量的方法;(3)明示或默示地规定货物的价格或确定价格的方法。《公约》只是规定了构成发盘的基本条件,在实际业务中,如果发盘的交易条件太少或过于简单,会给合同的履行带来困难,甚至容易引起争议。因此,在对外发盘时,最好将品名、质量、数量、价格、包装、保险、支付方式、装运等主要条款一一列明。

在国际业务中,有一类函电称为虚盘,虚盘是相对实盘而言。实盘是卖方按其所提供条件达成交易的肯定承诺,一旦买方在规定的期限内接受了报盘,卖方将不得对报盘中的任何条款做任何修改。虚盘是指对发盘的条件有保留或限制性条款,虚盘对卖方没有约束力。虚盘通常被视为邀请对方发盘,虚盘并不构成发盘。保留条款如:以我方最后确认为有效(subject to our final confirmation)、以货优先售出为有效(subject to prior sale)、本发盘无

约束力(offer without engagement)。限制性条款如：以认可装船样品为有效(subject to approval of shipping sample)、货物须由美国总统轮船公司承运(goods must be shipped through APL)。

Part II Letter Writing Guide

1. For general inquires 一般询盘信

(1) Telling addressee the source of information and making a brief self-introduction.

(2) Indicating the intention of writing the letter, i.e. to ask for a catalogue, samples or a pricelist.

(3) Stating the possibility of placing an order and expectation of an offer.

2. For specific inquires 具体询盘信

(1) Indicating the names and descriptions of the goods inquired for, including specifications, quantity, etc.

(2) Asking whether there is a possibility of giving a special discount and what terms of payment and time of delivery you would expect.

(3) Stating the possibility of placing an order and expectation of an offer.

3. For letter making offers 发盘信

(1) Expressing your thanks for the inquiry, if you've received one.

(2) Making an offer, stating all the details of the goods and the main terms of transaction as requested.

(3) Indicating the period for which the offer is valid if it is a firm offer, or remarking to the effect that the offer is made without engagement.

(4) Making favourable comments on the goods and the prices or drawing the customer's attention to other products likely to interest the buyer.

(5) Expressing your hope for an order.

Part Ⅲ Sample Letters

1. General Enquiries

 (1) A General Enquiry from a New Client

Dear Sirs,

We have noted from *China's Foreign Trade* that you manufacture a range of high-fashion blankets and would like to know whether you can supply us on FOB basis.

We are one of the leading importers in our country and have been handling textiles for about 20 years. Various kinds of blankets sell fast here, especially those fine in quality but low in price. We shall appreciate it if you will send us some brochures and particulars about your blankets so as to give us a general idea of their quality and designs.

If your goods and terms are satisfactory, we shall probably buy large quantities.

Yours faithfully,

×××

 (2) A Reply

Dear Sirs,

Thank you for your letter of November 14th, 2018 inquiring about our company and our products. Enclosed are our latest brochures as well as our financial statement for the year ending December 31st, 2017.

We are extending our business to the North American market, and hope to start our business with you. We would be happy to answer any questions that may arise after you read our brochures.

Yours faithfully,

×××

Notes

1. enquiry [in'kwaiəri] *n*. 询盘,询价

    general enquiry 一般询盘

    specific enquiry 具体询盘

    make/ send/ give sb. an enquiry for sth. 就某商品向某人询盘,向某人询问某商品

    e.g. We want to make an enquiry for 5,000 sets of Air Conditioner, Model No. KFR-26GW/101.

    我们想询问 5,000 台型号为 KFR-26GW/101 的空调的价格。

    enquire [in'kwai] *v*. 询盘,询价

    e.g. The goods you enquired for in your letter of May 15th are our best-sellers.

    你方 5 月 15 日信中所询商品是我们的畅销品。

2. supply [sə'plai] *v./n*. 供应,提供

    e.g. We are pleased to say that we can supply you with all the goods listed in your letter of July 4th.

    很高兴告诉贵方我们能够供应贵方 7 月 4 日来信中所列的所有货物。

    e.g. Owing to the shortage of raw materials, the goods are out of supply at present.

    由于原材料短缺,此货目前脱销。

    supplier [sə'plaiə] *n*. 供应商,供货商

    e.g. Suppliers and purchasers are the two counter parts in a transaction.

    供货商和购买方是一笔交易中的两个相对的当事人。

3. handle ['hændl] *vt*. 买卖,经营;触摸、搬运;对付、管理、控制(人、情况、机器等)

    (1) handle sth.: buy and sell sth. 买卖某物

    e.g. We have been handling the export of animal by products for more than ten year.

    我们经营动物副产品的出口超过 10 年了。

    e.g. This shop does not handle such goods.

    这家店不经营这类商品。

    (2) handle sth.: touch sth. with or hold sth. in the hands (用手)触、摸、拿、抓某物

    e.g. Fragile—handle with care.

    易碎品,小心轻放。

    (3) handle sth.: deal with, manage or control (people, a situation, a machine, etc.) 对付、管理、控制(人、情况、机器等)

    e.g. This port handles 100 million tons of cargo each year.

    这个港口每年货物吞吐量达 1 亿吨。

    e.g. I was impressed by her handling of the affair.

    我觉得她对此事的处理很了不起。

4. appreciate [ə'priʃieit] *vt*. be grateful for sth., feel gratitude 感谢,感激

    We would appreciate it if you would/ could ... 若能做某事……我们将不胜感激。

It will be appreciated if you would/ could … 若能做某事……我们将不胜感激。

We would appreciate sth. 我们感谢某事。

We would appreciate doing sth. 我们感谢做了某事。

e.g. We would appreciate it if you could send us your catalogue and price list.

如果能给我方寄来产品目录和价格单，我们将不胜感激。

e.g. It would be appreciated if you would send us samples of your new coffee tables.

若能寄来你方新款咖啡桌样品将不胜感激。

e.g. We really appreciate all the help you have given us.

感谢你给我们的种种帮助。

e.g. We shall appreciate your giving us some suggestions in this respect.

若能在这些方面给我们一些建议，我们将不胜感激。

5. particular [pəˈtikjulə] *n.* (often *pl.*) piece of information; detail; fact 信息；细节；事项

   e.g. He gave full particulars of the stolen property.

   他详细列出全部被盗的财物。

6. terms [tə:mz] *n.* (*pl.*) conditions offered or accepted（提出或接受的）条件

   according to the terms of the contract 按照合同的条件

7. inquire [inˈkwaiə] *v.* ask to be told sth.（by sb.）询问

   e.g. She inquired whether I wished to continue.

   她询问我是否想继续。

8. enclose [inˈkləuz] *vt.* 随函附寄

   e.g. I enclose the testing report issued by SGS for your reference.

   现随函附寄 SGS 的检测报告供参考。

9. financial statement 财务报告，财务报表

10. extend [iksˈtend] *vt.* make sth. longer or larger (in space or time) 使（某物）（在时间或空间上）更大、更长、延长、延展

    extend a fence, wall, railway, garden 扩建篱笆、墙、铁路、花园

    extend the market 扩大市场

11. arise [əˈraiz] *vi.* become evident; appear; originate 呈现；出现；发生

    e.g. A new difficulty has arisen.

    出现了新的困难。

    e.g. A storm arose during the night.

    夜间起了暴风雨。

(3) A General Enquiry from an Old Customer

Dear Mr. Black,

As we plan our fall inventory, we are again in the market to buy woolens. We are principally interested in the traditional sweater (men's and women's cardigans and pullovers), and would like to request a sample.

Please also send information on any other knitwear that your company produces and a current price list.

If you plan to have a representative at the Paris Trade Fair at the end of July, please advise us of your stand number so that we can contact you at that time.

Thank you for your attention.

Yours sincerely,

×××

 Notes

1. inventory [ˈɪnvəntɔːri] n. (North American English) all the goods in a shop (商店的)库存、存货 【同义】stock

   e.g. The inventory will be disposed of over the next twelve weeks.
   在未来的十二个星期将进行清仓处理。

2. woolens [ˈwulənz] n. (pl.) (esp. knitted) woolen garments (尤指针织的)毛织服装

   e.g. We stocked the shop up with woolens before winter.
   我们在入冬以前为商店备足毛织品。

3. principally [ˈprɪnsəpli] adv. mainly, chiefly 主要地；首要地；最重要地

   e.g. The economic system of the United States is principally one of private ownership.
   美国经济基本上是私有制经济。

4. cardigan [ˈkɑːdɪɡən] n. knitted woolen jacket, usu. with no collar and with buttons at the front (通常指无领有扣前对襟的)毛衣

   e.g. I'm looking for a size 39 woolen cardigan.
   我想买一件尺码39的羊毛开衫。

5. pullover [ˈpuləuvə] n. close-fitting knitted (esp. woolen) garment without fastenings, usu. worn over a shirt or blouse 针织(尤指毛织)紧身套衫(通常穿在衬衫外面) 【同义】

jersey, jumper, sweater

e.g. She wore a high-necked pullover to keep out the wind.

她穿一件高领套衫以御风寒。

6. knitwear ['nitweə] n. knitted garments 针织衣服

   e.g. The shop sells knitwear.

   这家商店出售针织品。

7. representative [ˌrepri'zentətiv] n. agent of a firm, esp. a travelling salesman（公司的）代理者;（尤指）派出的推销员;销售代表

   e.g. She's our representative in France.

   她是我们公司驻法国的销售代表。

8. trade fair: an exhibition at which many different companies show and sell their products 商品交易会,商品展销会

   e.g. We should take advantage of the trade fair to advertise our products.

   我们要好好利用这次商品交易会来宣传我们的产品。

9. advise [əd'vaiz] vt. advise sb. (of sth.) (esp. commerce) inform or notify sb. （尤用于商业）通知或告知某人

   e.g. Please advise us of the dispatch of the goods.

   货物发出请通知我们。

10. stand [stænd] n. area or structure where things are displayed, exhibited, advertised, etc. 摊位(用于陈列、展览、宣传等目的)

    a display/ an exhibition/ a trade stand 展位;展销台

11. attention [ə'tenʃən] n. special care or action; practical consideration 特别的照顾或处理;实际的考虑

    e.g. This letter is for the attention of the manager.

    这封信是要经理亲自处理的。

2. Specific Enquiries

（1）A Specific Enquiry about Computer Keyboard

Dear Sirs,

One of our customers is interested in your "Light" Brand Wireless Bluetooth Computer Keyboard and asks us to approach you for quotations and samples.

The market here for computer and its components is enormous. Please quote us your lowest price CIF Shanghai for 7,500 pieces of Art. No. FK-990, indicating the earliest date of shipment and payment terms.

Besides, we would also appreciate it if you could send us a copy of your export list regarding all the goods you are dealing in so that we can contact you at any time when there is a demand.

Yours faithfully,

×××

 Notes

1. specific [spəˈsifik] *adj*. detailed, precise and exact 详细而精确的；确切的

   e.g. The description of your goods should be specific and concrete.
   货物的描述必须明确具体。

2. brand [brænd] *n*. trade mark of goods 商品的牌子；商标

   e.g. The developed markets impose higher requirements on brand and we are focusing our efforts on enhancing our brand management.
   发达市场对品牌的要求很高，目前我们致力于加强品牌管理。

3. wireless bluetooth computer keyboard 无线蓝牙计算机键盘

4. approach [əˈprəutʃ] *v*. go to (sb.) for help or support or in order to offer sth. 接近某人或某事 come near or nearer to sb./sth. on space or time（在空间或时间上）接近，靠近（某人或某事）

   e.g. Mr. Holland has approached that bank several times for loan.
   霍兰德先生已就贷款一事多次联系那家银行。

   e.g. As the production is approaching completion, you are requested to fax us as early as possible.
   由于生产接近尾声，请尽快传真与我们联系。

5. quotation [kwəuˈteiʃən] *n*. 报价

   quotation sheet 报价单

   make/ send/ give sb. a quotation for sth. 给某人报某商品价格

   e.g. We look forward to receiving your best quotation CFR London for 4,000 reams of quality art printing paper.
   请报4,000令优质铜版纸最低成本加运费伦敦价。

   quote [kwəut] *v*. 报价

   quote sb. a price for/ on sth. 给某人报某商品价格

   e.g. Please quote us your lowest price and the date of delivery.
   请给我方最低报价并告知交货日期。

6. Art. No. (article number) 货号

   article [ˈaːtikl] *n*. a particular item or separate thing (esp. one of a set) 物件，物品（尤指整套中的一件）

   e.g. We can supply our customers with this kind of article at a reasonable price.
   我们能以合理的价格向顾客供应这类商品。

7. deal in 经营

   e.g. Chinese small-sized and medium-sized non-governmental enterprises mainly deal in light industrial products, textiles and daily necessaries.
   中国中小型民营企业主要经营轻工业品、纺织品和日用品。

8. contact [ˈkɔntækt] *n*. communication 通讯；联系；交往　[kʌnˈtækt] *vt*. reach (sb./sth.) by telephone, radio, letter, etc.; communicate with 与某人或某事联系，与……来往

   in contact with sb. 与某人保持联系

   e.g. We contact you for your comments on our new products.
   我们想知道你们对我们新产品的意见。

   e.g. We should stay in contact with former clients for further opportunities.
   为了更多的机会，我们应该和以前的客户保持联系。

9. demand [diˈmænd] *n*. demand for sth./sb., desire of customers for goods or services which they wish to buy or use （客户的）需求，需要　*vt*. ask for sth. as if one is commanding or as if one has the right to do so 要求，请求（某事物）

   e.g. There is a large demand for our washing machine in the African market.
   非洲市场对我们的洗衣机有大量的需求。

   e.g. They demand that we go and meet them in Guangzhou at the beginning of next month.
   他们要求我们下月初去广州与他们见面。

（2）A Reply When Stock Is Not Available

Dear Mr. Bean,

　　Your inquiry of August 8th, 2018, has been well received. Thank you very much for your interest in our "Light" Brand Wireless Bluetooth Computer Keyboard.

　　We regret very much to inform you that we are not in a position, owing to heavy orders, to supply you with the said goods. We shall be pleased to revert to this matter once our supplies are available.

We look forward to doing business with you soon in the future.

Yours sincerely,

×××

 Notes

1. in a position to do 能够做某事

    e.g. I am in a position to save you a good deal of time.

    我能够为你节省许多时间。

2. owing to: because of or on account of sth. 由于,因为

    e.g. Owing to the rain, the match was cancelled.

    比赛因雨取消了。

3. revert [ri'və:t] v. return to (a topic in talk or thought) 回到(原话题或思路)

    e.g. The conversation kept reverting to the subject of money.

    谈话的内容一再回到钱的问题。

 (3) A Specific Enquiry in Reply to a Product Recommendation Letter

Dear Sirs,

Thank you for your email of June 18th. We note with pleasure that you intend to develop business with us in the line of textiles.

We have gone through your catalogue and find that cotton Table-Cloths Art. No. 120 and 130 are of interest to us. We shall be pleased if you could quote us the lowest price in pound sterling CIFC 5% Port Manchester. Please also indicate the quantities of the various sizes that you can supply for prompt delivery. If your prices are reasonable and quantities satisfactory, we shall consider placing substantial orders.

We have handled table-cloth for more than ten years and have good connections all over the country. We have also some associated firms in West European countries, where we may find a ready market for your products as well.

We trust you will give this enquiry your immediate attention and let us have your reply at an early date.

Sincerely yours,

×××

Notes

1. note [nəut] vt. notice sth.; observe 注意(某事物);观察

    e.g. Please note that the office will be closed on Monday.

    请注意办事处星期一将关闭。

2. line [lain] n. type of product (产品的)类型,种类

    e.g. We are starting a new line in casual clothes.

    我们将着手经营新款式的休闲装。

    e.g. Some lines sell better than others.

    有些品种的货物销售得好些,有些则较差。

3. be of interest to sb.; be interesting to sb. 令某人产生兴趣的

    e.g. The subject is of no interest to me at all.

    我对此课题一点都不感兴趣。

4. sterling ['stə:liŋ] n. British money 英国货币

    payable in sterling or American dollars 用英镑或美元支付

5. Manchester [mæn'tʃəstə] n. 曼彻斯特(英国英格兰西北部港市),世界上最早的工业化城市,英国重要的交通枢纽,商业、金融、工业、文化中心。

6. substantial [sʌb'stænʃl] adj. large in amount; considerable 数目大的,可观的,大量的

    e.g. Her contribution to the discussion was substantial.

    她在讨论中做了很多工作。

7. handle ['hændl] vt. buy and sell (sth.) 买卖(某物)

    e.g. This shop does not handle such goods.

    这家商店不经营这类商品。

3. Firm Offers

 (1) An Offer in List Form

Dear Sirs,

We are in receipt of your inquiry dated March 21st and we take pleasure in making you a special offer as follows:

Art. No.: 81000 Printed Shirting

Design No.: 72435-2A

Specifications: 30×36×72×69 36″×42yds

Quantity: 12,600 yards

Packing: in bales or in wooden cases, at seller's option

48

Price: US$ 34 per yard CIFC 5% Vancouver

Shipment: to be made in three equal monthly installments, beginning from June, 2020

Payment: by confirmed, irrevocable L/C payable by draft at sight to be opened 30 days before the time of shipment

We trust the above will be acceptable to you and await your trial order with keen interest.

Yours faithfully,

× × ×

 Notes

1. be in receipt of 已收到

    e.g. We are in receipt of your enquiry for 50 sets Sewing Machines. = We have received your enquiry for 50 sets Sewing Machines.

    我们已收到你方就 500 套缝纫机的询盘。

2. take/ have pleasure in doing sth. (某人)很高兴(做某事) 【同义】take/ have the pleasure of doing sth.; take/ have the pleasure to do sth.

    e.g. We take the pleasure of telling you that we have accepted your offer of November 15th for 500 sets of computer keyboard and mouse.

    我们很高兴地通知你方我们已经接受了你方 11 月 15 日 500 套电脑键盘和鼠标的发盘。

3. Art. No. (article number) 商品编号,货号。指在目录本或样品本里某一商品的编号,在报价时写明货号,以免误解。

4. option ['ɔpʃən] n. power or freedom of choosing; choice 选择权;选择自由;选择

    at seller's option 由卖方选择

    at buyer's option 由买方选择

    e.g. This particular model comes with a wide range of options.

    这一种型号的货物有很多选择。

5. CIFC 5% Vancouver 到温哥华的 CIF 价含佣金 5%

    这里第二个 C 指的是 commission,佣金。

6. installment [in'stɔːlmənt] n. any one of the parts of the payment spread over a period of time 分期付款,分批装运

    three equal monthly installments 按月分三等批装运

    e.g. How many installments did it take to pay off the loan?

    需要分几期还清贷款?

7. await [əˈweit] v. wait for (sb./sth.) 等候,等待 sb. await sth. = sb. wait for sth.

   e.g. We await your early reply.

   我们期待你的早日回复。

8. trial order 试订,试购

   e.g. We suggest your placing a trial order to see how it goes.

   我们建议你试订购看看如何。

9. keen [ki:n] adj. (of feelings, etc.) intense; strong; deep (指感情等)热烈的、强烈的、深刻的

   with keen interest 殷切的

   a keen desire, interest, sense of loss 强烈的愿望、兴趣、失落感

（2）An Offer in the Paragraph Form

Dear Sirs,

Groundnuts & Walnut meat

We confirm your letter of September 2nd asking us to make you offers for both Groundnuts and Walnut meat CFR Copenhagen. In reply, we are offering you 350 metric tons of Groundnuts, Hand-picked, Shelled and Upgraded at USD 1,300 net per metric ton CFR Copenhagen or any other European Main Port for shipment during October/November, 2018. This offer is valid, subject to the receipt of reply reaching us before September 25th.

Please note that we have offered our most favourable price and are unable to entertain any counter-offer.

As regards Walnut meat, the few parcels we have at present are under offer elsewhere. However, if you should make us an acceptable bid, there is a possibility of your obtaining them.

As you are aware that there has been lately a large demand for the above commodities, such growing demand has doubtlessly resulted in increased prices. However, you may take the advantage of this strengthening market if you send us an immediate reply.

Yours truly,

× × ×

Notes

1. confirm [kənˈfəːm] v. provide evidence for the truth or correctness of (a report, an opinion, etc.); establish the truth of 证实,证明;确认

    e.g. We confirm receipt of your letter of May 5th.

    我们确认收到你方5月5日来信。

2. firm [fəːm] adj. not subject to change; definite 不易改变的、肯定的;坚定的

    firm offer 实盘 non-firm offer 虚盘

    e.g. This offer is firm, subject to your reply by 5 p.m. our time, Wednesday, October 3rd.

    该发盘为实盘,以你方在我方时间10月3日星期三下午5点前回复为有效。

3. EMP (European Main Ports) 欧洲主要口岸

4. favourable [ˈfeivərəbl] adj. 有利的;赞成的

    favourable price 有利的价格,优惠的价格

    e.g. We are favourable of your proposal.

    我们赞成你的提议。

    e.g. The time is not favourable for the disposal of the goods.

    这个时间对于处理这批货物并不利。

5. entertain [ˌentəˈtein] v. be ready and willing to consider sth. 考虑接受(某事物)

    e.g. We shall be glad to entertain any constructive suggestion you make.

    我们将很乐意考虑你的建设性意见。

    e.g. We are too heavily committed to be able to entertain fresh orders.

    我们订单太多而无法考虑新的订单。

6. parcel [ˈpɑːsl] n. thing or things wrapped up for carrying or sending by post 包裹,小包;一批货

    e.g. We are sending you a parcel of samples.

    我们给你寄去了一包样品。

7. under offer 在出售中

    e.g. We have only a parcel of 100 tons left, which is under offer elsewhere.

    我们只有一批100吨的货,该货现在正在别处出售中。

8. bid [bid] n. price offered in order to buy sth., esp. at an auction 出价(尤指拍卖时)

    v. offer (a price) in order to buy sth., esp. at an auction (购物时)出价,(尤指拍卖时)喊价

    e.g. If we ask the buyers for a bid, probably they will name a low price.

    如果我们要求买方出价,他们很有可能给出一个低价。

    e.g. They made a bid at US $ 1,300 net per metric ton CFR Copenhagen for walnut meat.

    他们给核桃仁出的价是成本加运费至哥本哈根每公吨1,300美元。

9. aware [əˈwɛə] adj. having knowledge or realization of sb./sth. 意识到的;知道的

e.g. We are fully aware of the change in the market.

我们完全意识到市场的变化。

e.g. We are not aware of why you have not opened the L/C.

我们不知道你们为什么还没有开立信用证。

10. lately ['leitli] *adv*. in recent times; recently 最近；不久前

 e.g. We have received a crowd of enquiries lately.

 我们最近收到很多询盘。

11. result in 导致

 e.g. We confirm cables exchanged resulting in the sale to you of 15 metric tons licorice.

 我们确认电报往来中达成的向你方出售15公吨甘草的交易。

 result from 产生于

 e.g. We confirm the sale to you of 15 metric tons licorice resulting from letters exchanged.

 我们确认信件往来中产生的向你方出售15公吨甘草的交易。

12. strengthen ['streŋθn] *vt*. to become stronger; to make sb./sth. stronger 加强　　*vi*. 价格上涨

 e.g. We agree to your proposed terms for this transaction in order to strengthen our relations.

 为了加强我们的关系，我们同意你关于这笔交易所提的条件。

 e.g. The market is strengthening.

 市场正在增强。

（3）A Firm Offer in Chart Form

Dear Mr. Paul Smith,

We acknowledge with thanks the receipt of your letter dated September 15th, showing your interest in toy bears and extending the wish to place large orders with us.

In reply, we are offering you as follows:

COMMODITY	ARTICLE NO.	PACKING	CARTONS PER 20' FCL	CIFC 3% TORONTO (USD)
BROWN BEAR	KB001	8 SETS/CTN	135	13.65 PER SET
BEAR IN BALLET COSTUME	KB002	12 PCS/CTN	162	8.12 PER PC
PLUSH TWIN BEAR	KB003	4 SETS/CTN	213	14.61 PER SET
TOY BEAR IN SWEATER	KB004	8 PCS/CTN	302	9.89 PER PC

Shipment: to be effected within 2 months after receipt of the relevant L/C

Payment: by sight L/C

Insurance: for 110% invoice value covering ALL RISKS and WAR RISK

Under separate cover, we have sent you samples of various kinds and the catalogue required. I'm sure you will find that our products are of excellent quality and favorable price.

This offer is valid for 7 days.

We look forward to receiving your detailed requirements.

Yours faithfully,

×××

 Notes

1. extend [ik'stend] vt. extend sth. (to sb.); offer or give sth. 提供或给予某事物

   extend hospitality/ an invitation/ a greeting to sb. 款待/邀请/问候某人

2. FCL (Full Container Load) 整箱装集装箱

   LCL (Less Container Load) 拼箱装集装箱

3. ballet ['bælei] n. style of dancing used to tell a story in a dramatic performance with music but without speech or singing 芭蕾舞

   ballet shoes 芭蕾舞鞋

4. costume ['kɔstju:m] n. garment or style of dress (esp. of a particular peroid or group or for a particular activity) 服装;服装样式(尤指用于某时期、某团体或某活动的)

   swimming costume 游泳衣

   skiing costume 滑雪服

5. effect [i'fect] vt. bring sth. about; cause to occur (使)某事物产生;(使)发生

   effect a change/ a sale/ shipment 引起变化/实行大减价/安排装运

6. cover ['kʌvə] vt. include (sth.); deal with 包括(某事物);涉及;处理;适用于

   the salesman covering the northern part of the country 负责该国北部地区促销的推销员

   e.g. Do the rules cover a case like this?

   这些规则是否适用于这样的情况?

7. under separate cover 另封邮寄 【同义】by separate post

4. A Non-firm Offer

Dear Sirs,

We thank you for your letter dated April 8th inquiring for leather handbags. As requested, we take pleasure in offering you, subject to our final confirmation, 300 dozen of deerskin handbags style No. MA 190 at $ 124.00 per dozen CIF Hamburg. Shipment will be effected within 25 days after receipt of the relevant L/C issued by your first class bank in our favour upon signing Sales Contract.

We are manufacturing various kinds of leather purses and waist-belts for export, and under separate cover, a brochure of products and samples have been sent to you by airmail today. We hope some of them would meet your customers' taste and need.

If we can be of any further help, please feel free to let us know. Customers' inquiries always meet with our careful attention. We await with keen interest your order.

Yours faithfully,

× × ×

 Notes

1. deerskin ['diəskin] *n*. (leather made of) deer's skin 鹿皮

    e.g. In comparison to other leathers, deerskin offers comparatively high tensile strength.

    与其他皮革相比,鹿革有更高的拉伸强度。

2. in one's favour 以某人为受益人

    e.g. We have opened an L/C in your favour through the Bank of China for the amount of US$ 180,000.

    我们已通过中国银行开立了以你方为受益人的金额为 180,000 美元的信用证。

3. waist-belt ['weistbelt] *n*. 腰带;束腰带

    e.g. Unbuckle your pack's waist-belt before starting.

    开始前请解开你的背包腰带。

Part Ⅳ Useful Expressions and Sentences

Expressions

1. general enquiry 一般询盘
2. specific enquiry 具体询盘
3. make/send/give sb. an enquiry for sth. 就某商品向某人询盘, 向某人询问某商品
4. financial statement 财务报告, 财务报表
5. trade fair 商品交易会；商品展销会
6. advise sb. (of sth.) 通知或告知某人(某事)
7. quotation sheet 报价单
8. make/ send/ give sb. a quotation for sth. 给某人报某商品价格
9. article number 货号
10. deal in 经营
11. in a position to do 能够做某事
12. owing to：because of or on account of sth. 由于, 因为
13. be in receipt of 已收到
14. (sb.) take/ have pleasure in doing sth. （某人）很高兴(做某事)
15. at seller's option 由卖方选择
16. trial order 试订, 试购
17. firm offer 实盘
18. non-firm offer 虚盘
19. under separate cover 另封邮寄
20. in one's favour 以某人为受益人

Typical Sentences

1. We need all necessary information regarding your products available for export now.
2. Please study the samples carefully and send us your CFR price.
3. We would also like to know the quantities needed for each color and design.
4. Could you give us detailed description of the performance of your product?
5. We would like to take this opportunity to inquire about the price of tennis racket.
6. The goods are available subject to your acceptance here before May 23rd, 2019.
7. We'd like to inform you that our counter sample will be sent to you by DHL by

the end of this week. Please confirm it ASAP so that we can start mass production.

8. The offer is valid until June 2nd, after which date the terms and prices should be discussed again.

9. The goods you enquire for can be supplied within one month after receipt of your order.

10. We can supply bicycles according to the specifications indicated in your letter of September 8th.

Part Ⅴ   Practical Training

Ⅰ. Elementary Training

1. Choose the best answer.

(1) We thank you for your letter of March 12th and the ____ catalogue.

  A. sent   B. enclosed   C. given   D. presented

(2) The letter we sent last week is an enquiry ____ color TV sets.

  A. about   B. for   C. of   D. as

(3) If you are interested, we will send you a sample lot ____ charge.

  A. within   B. with   C. for   D. free of

(4) While ____ an enquiry, you ought to enquire about quality, specification and price, etc.

  A. making   B. offering   C. sending   D. giving

(5) They found an opportunity to purchase six ____ leather shoes.

  A. thousands pairs   B. thousand pairs

  C. thousands of pair   D. thousand pairs of

(6) What kind of products do you think ____ particularly interested ____?

  A. are they, in   B. they are, in   C. are they, /   D. they are, /

(7) It may interest you to know that there is a good demand here for Chinese Black Tea ____ prices.

  A. at moderate   B. in cheap   C. for low   D. on dear

(8) Please reply as soon as possible, ____ the earliest shipment date and terms of payment.

  A. stated   B. as stated   C. stating   D. state

(9) We enquire ____ glassware available ____ export.

    A. for, to   B. for, for   C. to, for   D. of, about

(10) We are pleased ____ your enquiry of July 15th for our toys.

    A. to receiving   B. as received   C. receiving   D. to have

(11) We would not give you any lower price ____ you could place an order for more than 500 tons.

    A. expect   B. until   C. unless   D. besides

(12) There is a steady demand in Europe ____ leather gloves ____ high quality.

    A. for, with   B. for, of   C. at, with   D. in, of

(13) We ____ some brochures ____ to illustrate the types of materials we manufacture.

    A. enclose you, /   B. enclose, you

    C. enclose, /   D. enclose, to you

(14) They have ____ us that you are ____ the market ____ chemical.

    A. inform, in, on   B. informed, in, for

    C. advise, in, on   D. advise, in, of

(15) For your information, our products enjoy a ready ____ in Europe.

    A. sell   B. sale   C. selling   D. sail

(16) We have been approached ____ several buyers for the supply of HV switchgear.

    A. by   B. with   C. as   D. for

(17) We would recommend you ____ this offer.

    A. accept   B. accepted   C. to accept   D. accepting

(18) Thank you for your letter of December 20th, ____ which you offered us 12,500 yards of printed shirting on the following terms and conditions.

    A. from   B. of   C. in   D. to

(19) Our price is more attractive as ____ that offered by suppliers elsewhere.

    A. compared to   B. compared with

    C. compare to   D. compare with

(20) We are not in a position to offer firm, as goods are ____ .

    A. without stock   B. outside in stock

    C. no stock   D. out of stock

(21) ____ we would like to close the business with you, we find your price unacceptable.

    A. Much   B. However much

    C. Much as   D. Despite

(22) Please let us ____ your firm offer before the end of this month.

    A. has   B. have   C. having   D. to have

(23) ____ we thank you for your enquiry, we regret being unable to make you an offer for the time being.

  A. While   B. When   C. As   D. Since

(24) We are offering you goods ____ high quality.

  A. of   B. at   C. for   D. with

(25) A firm offer ____ a time limit for acceptance.

  A. may specify   B. never specifies

  C. sometimes specifies   D. must specify

(26) If you can ____ your price by 5%, we may conclude the transaction with you.

  A. offer   B. bring down   C. fix   D. quote

(27) The commodities you offered are ____ line with the business scope of our clients.

  A. outside   B. out   C. out of   D. without

(28) We are offering you firm ____ on the same terms and conditions as the previous contract.

  A. as following   B. as follow   C. as is following   D. as follows

2. Read the following letters and fill in each blank with prepositions.

Letter 1

Dear Sirs,

Iron Nails

We are interested __(1)__ buying large quantities of Iron Nails __(2)__ all sizes and would be thankful if you could give us a quotation per metric ton CIF Lagos, Nigeria.

It would also be appreciated if samples and a brochure could be forwarded to us.

We used to purchase this article from other sources but we now prefer to buy from your corporation because we are given to understand that you are able to supply larger quantities __(3)__ more attractive prices. Besides, we have confidence __(4)__ the quality of Chinese products.

We look forward to hearing __(5)__ you by return.

Yours sincerely,

×××

Letter 2

Dear Sirs,

We acknowledge __(1)__ thanks the receipt of your letter dated March 11th inquiring about the possibility of selling your men's shirts, Tiantan Brand, in our market.

__(2)__ reply, we wish to inform you that we are well connected __(3)__ major dealers in the line of textiles. There is always a ready market here __(4)__ men's shirts, provided they are of good quality and competitive in price. Therefore, it will be appreciated if you will let us have your best firm offer, preferably by fax, and send us samples by airmail. If your shirts agree __(5)__ the taste of our market, we feel confident of placing a trial order with you.

Please give this inquiry your prompt attention.

Yours sincerely,

×××

Letter 3

Dear Sirs,

We confirm having received your inquiry of August 20th __(1)__ our gold pens CIF London. Complying __(2)__ your request, we are making you a firm offer as follows:

Commodity: Seagull Brand Gold Pens

Specification: As per attached list

Quantity: 1,000 dozen

Packing: In cartons of 100 dozen each

Price: __(3)__ £ 24 per dozen CIFC 5% London

Shipment: During October/ November, 2019.

Payment: __(4)__ confirmed, irrevocable L/C

This offer is firm, subject __(5)__ your reply reaching us before September 1st.

Please note that we have offered you our most favorable price and thus we are unable

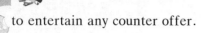

to entertain any counter offer.

We are hoping that you will accept our offer as soon as possible.

Yours faithfully,

×××

Letter 4

Dear Sirs,

Thank you for your letter of September 15th, 2019, and the inquiry enclosed for our White Rabbit pajamas.

At your request, we are making you a firm offer __(1)__ 20,000 dozen women's pajamas at USD 48.5 per dz. CFRC 5% Lagos __(2)__ shipment in March, 2019. Payment is to be made by confirmed, irrevocable L/C payable __(3)__ draft __(4)__ sight. This offer is firm subject to your reply reaching us within one week. The relevant sample and catalog have been sent __(5)__ separate mail. Please note all the prices quoted are bottom prices and no counter-offer will be accepted. If you agree to the above, please make confirmation as soon as possible so as to enable us to make the necessary arrangements.

We are looking forward to your early reply.

Yours sincerely,

×××

 3. Translate the following English into Chinese.

(1) make/ send/ give sb. an enquiry for sth.

(2) financial statement

(3) advise sb. (of sth.)

(4) make/ send/ give sb. a quotation for sth.

(5) in a position to do

(6) owing to

(7) be in receipt of

(8) take/ have pleasure in doing sth.

(9) trial order

(10) under separate cover

(11) We need all necessary information regarding your products available for export now.

(12) We very much appreciate the special quotation you sent us on March 18th.

(13) Some of our customers have recently expressed interest in your woolen carpets and inquired about their quality and prices.

(14) In reply to your inquiry, we are pleased in making you the following offer.

(15) We are making you a firm offer of 30 metric tons walnut meat at EUR 2,500 per metric ton CIF European main ports for November shipment.

(16) We are making you the following offer, subject to your acceptance reaching us not later than September 15th, 2018.

(17) This offer will remain firm until March 31st, 2018, beyond which date the terms and prices should be discussed anew.

(18) The offer is subject to our final confirmation.

(19) Owing to the increased demand for this type of car, our stocks have run very low.

(20) As prices are steadily rising we would advise you to place your order without delay.

Ⅱ. Intermediate Training

1. Supply the missing words in the blanks of the following letter. The first letters are given.

Dear Madam or Sir,

We have read your a_____ in *International Trade* and are glad to know that you are one of the l_____ exporters of silk blouses in China. We are i_____ in the goods and would like to be informed of the d_____ of your various types, including sizes, colors and prices.

We are large d_____ in silk garments, having over 15 years' experience in this particular l_____ of business. Silk blouses of good quality and moderate prices enjoy a good sale(销路好,畅销) in our m_____.

When r____, please state the terms of payment and the discounts you would allow on purchases of o____ 100 dozen individual i____.

We look forward to your early reply.

Yours sincerely,

×××

2. Cloze. Choose the most suitable words form the list of words to fill in the blanks. Each word can be used only once.

quotation   receipt   confirmation   discount   catalogues

inquiring   appreciated   subject   separate   brochures

Dear Sirs,

Thank you for your letter of March 6th, 2020, __(1)__ for our tape recorders and your desire to enter into direct business relations with us.

As requested, we are sending you our __(2)__ sheet covering the types in which you are interested. Unless otherwise stated, all the products can be supplied within four weeks after the __(3)__ of your order. The prices listed are __(4)__ to our final __(5)__. On an order exceeding 10,000 sets, we usually allow a 3% quantity __(6)__.

Some latest __(7)__ and __(8)__ have also been sent to you under __(9)__ cover for your reference. Should any of the items be suitable for your market, please let us know. As soon as your specific inquiry is received, we will make you an offer immediately.

Your early reply will be much __(10)__.

×××

3. Translate the following Chinese into English.
(1) 一般询盘
(2) 具体询盘
(3) 商品交易会
(4) 报价单

(5) 货号

(6) 由卖方选择

(7) 实盘

(8) 虚盘

(9) 经营

(10) 以某人为受益人

(11) 感谢你方 4 月 20 日对我方篮球的询价。

(12) 请告知能否在 4 月份向我方供应一万只水表(water meter)。

(13) 如能寄来最新价格单和样品供我方参考,将不胜感激。

(14) 我方想了解你方的交易条款。

(15) 只有质优价廉的产品才能吸引我方客户。

(16) 以上报价均为不含佣金的净价。

(17) 鉴于你方是我们的老客户,我们同意按你方的价格供货。

(18) 根据你方要求,现报价如下。

(19) 货物的品质必须与样品完全一致。

(20) 收到样品后,请尽快确认以便我们安排生产。

Ⅲ. Advanced Training

 Translate the following letter into English.

敬启者:

你方于 6 月 15 日来信及信中所附对我公司白兔牌睡衣的询盘收悉。

按照你方要求,现报 20,000 打女式睡衣,成本加运费含 5% 佣金至拉各斯价每打 48.5 美元,2019 年 8 月装船,以保兑的、不可撤销的信用证凭即期汇票支付。本报盘以你方一周内复到为有效。

请注意所报价格均为底价,不接受任何还盘。请尽快确认,以便我方安排有关事宜。

盼早复。

×××谨上

Unit 4　Counter-offer
还　　盘

Lead-in

Try to finish the following tasks and find out the learning objectives of this unit.

Task 1

假设你是英国富兰克林贸易公司（Franklin Trading Co. Ltd.；Address：15 Newell Street，London，Britain；Tel：0044-20-76812345；Fax：0044-20-76757890；Email：Franklin@hotmail.com）进口部的经理。最近，你公司收到广州金发鞋业公司（Guangzhou Jinfa Shoes Company；Address：138 Yanjiang Road，Guangzhou，China；Tel：86-20-66668888；Fax：86-20-66788889；Email：jinfa89@163.com）发来的关于 CDM 牌鞋子的实盘。你们对该公司的报价不满意，打算就价格方面的问题与其磋商。现在，请代表公司拟一封还盘函。注意信中务必包含以下内容：

（1）感谢贵公司 8 月 1 日给予我方 200 双 CDM 牌鞋子成本加保险费、运费至利物浦（Liverpool）每双 45 欧元的报价。

（2）很遗憾我们无法按贵方价格成交，因为贵方价格与市场不一致。同等品质的鞋子，本地的百货公司零售价格低很多。

（3）鉴于我们之间长期的贸易关系，我们愿意给你们一个还盘，希望贵方可以将价格降低 10 欧元。

（4）如果贵方能接受我们的还盘，我们将会考虑订购 300 双。

（5）希望贵方对我们的还盘给予认真的考虑并在北京时间 2019 年 8 月 10 日下午 5 点前答复我方。

（6）盼佳音。

Task 2

假设你是中国梦露国际贸易有限公司(Monroe International Trading Company Ltd.；Address：Room 10，36 Yudao Road，Nanjing，P. R. China；Tel：86-25-67117890)销售部的经理。最近，你公司收到美国立浦特国际贸易公司(Liput International Trading Co.，Ltd.；Address：118 West Street，New York，U.S.A.；Tel：001-212-5412888)发来的关于棉质长裤的还盘。虽然你们对该宗交易的价格条件不是很满意，但考虑到双方长期友好的合作关系，还是打算破例接受该还盘。现在，请代表公司拟一封接受函。注意信中务必包含以下内容：

(1) 很高兴收到贵公司12月9日关于棉质长裤(cotton pants)的订单。

(2) 虽然我们对该宗交易的价格条件不是很满意，但考虑到双方长期友好的合作关系，还是打算破例接受该还盘。

(3) 现确认按贵方函电中所开列的如下条件供应棉质长裤：

价格：每条南京装运港码头交货价11美元

数量：200条

包装：按贵方指示包装(according to your instructions)

装运：2019年3月1日前从南京发往纽约。

支付：凭至少在交货日期前30天开立的、保兑的、不可撤销的信用证以即期汇票支付

(4) 我们保证按合同规定执行贵方订单，相信你们收到货物后，一定会感到非常满意。

(5) 很高兴这次能与贵公司达成交易。相信我们的首次交易将促成双方日后更多、更重要的贸易往来。

Part Ⅰ Introduction

如果买方不同意报价或报盘中的某些交易条件，包括价格、支付条件、交货期、起订量等，他可以发出还盘或还价。

在还盘中，买方可以就某些交易条件提出异议并陈述自己的建议。这样的变更，不管多么微不足道，都意味着交易要在新的基础上重新谈判。原来的发盘人卖方现在成了受盘人，完全有权利接受或拒绝还盘。在后一种情况下，他也可以在买方还盘的基础上发自己的还盘。还盘的过程可以进行很多回合直到达成交易或取消交易。

关于还盘的函电主要涉及以下内容：

1. 价格谈判。买卖双方对某一物或某一事就双方共同关心的价格问题互相磋商，交换意见，寻求解决的途径，找到双方都能接受的价格范围，最终达成协议的过程。

2. 拒绝还盘。受盘人对发盘条件不同意，表示无法满足对方要求，并同时明确说明拒

绝的原因。

3. 接受还盘。受盘人完全同意发盘条件或条款,接受还盘。

4. 订单的部分拒绝。出口商对订单中某些要求无法满足,表明拒绝,并提出替代方案。

Part Ⅱ Letter Writing Guide

1. For letters of price negotiation 价格谈判

    (1) Thanking the offeror for his offer.

    (2) Expressing regret at inability to accept the offer and giving reasons for non-acceptance.

    (3) Making a counter-offer if, in the circumstances, it is appropriate.

    (4) Expressing your hope and expectation.

2. For letters declining a counter-offer 拒绝还盘

    (1) Expressing your thanks for the counter-offer and surprise at the counter-offer.

    (2) Refusing to accept counter-offer and stating the reason.

    (3) Hoping that the counter-offer will be revised as soon as possible so as to leave room for possible future trade transactions.

3. For letters of acceptance of a counter-offer 接受还盘

    (1) Thanking the senders for their offers or counter-offers.

    (2) Declaring that you accept the counter-offer from the senders. State that you would like to conclude business with the senders according to the terms and conditions agreed upon. (List all the terms and conditions agreed upon in detail.)

    (3) Stating that you have enclosed an Order Form/ Contract/ Sales Confirmation, asking for the returning of one copy duly signed for your file. (It may be not necessary if a signed copy is not needed.)

    (4) Expressing your hope that the transaction would be conducted smoothly and successfully and that business would be expanded in the future.

4. For letters of partial rejection of an order 订单的部分拒绝

    (1) Expressing your thanks for receiving the order.

    (2) Expressing regret at inability to accept the order and giving reasons for non-acceptance.

    (3) Proposing a substitution for consideration.

Part Ⅲ   Sample Letters

1. Price Negotiation

 （1）Counter-offer on Nut Kernels

Dear Sirs,

<u>Nut Kernels FAQ 2019 Crop</u>

We are in receipt of your letter of July 22nd offering us 100 metric tons of the captioned goods at US$ 1,200 per metric ton on usual terms.

In reply, we regret to inform you that our buyers in Rotterdam find your price much too high. Information indicates that some parcels of Indian origin have been sold here at a level about 10% lower than yours.

We do not deny that the quality of Chinese nut kernels is slightly better, but the difference in price should, in no case, be as big as 10%. To step up the trade, we counter-offer as follows, subject to your reply received by us on or before August 15th:

100 metric tons of nut kernels FAQ 2019 crop.

At US$ 1,100 per m/t CIF Rotterdam.

Other terms as per your letter of July 22nd.

As the market is declining, we recommend your immediate acceptance.

Yours faithfully,

×××

 Notes

1. FAQ (2019 Crop) (2019年收成的)大路货

FAQ 是 Fair Average Quality 的缩写,也可以写作 F.A.Q. 或 faq/ f.a.q.,译为良好平均品质,我们习惯上称为大路货,常作为出口农副产品的品质标准。

2. on (the) usual terms 按照惯常条款

   e.g. We are pleased to have concluded business on usual terms.

   我们很高兴按照惯常条款达成交易。

3. indicate [ˈindikeit] v. 指出；表明；说明

   e.g. Please make us an offer, indicating the best possible shipment.

   请报盘，说明最好的装运方式。

   e.g. Information indicates that our new products are in great demand.

   信息表明我们的新产品需求量很大。

4. origin [ˈɒridʒin] n. 产地

   country of origin 生产国别

   e.g. Certificate of Origin is required.

   需要原产地证书。

5. level [ˈlevl] n. 水平，本为"水平"，常引申为"价格"

   e.g. Your price is not on a level with the current market.

   你方价格与当前市场不符。

   e.g. We shall appreciate it if you will place orders with us at something near our level.

   如果你方能以接近我方的价格向我方订货，我们将不胜感激。

   e.g. We have closed business at this level with buyers at your end.

   我们已在这一级别与你方买家达成交易。

6. deny [diˈnai] v. 否认；拒绝承认

   e.g. It cannot be denied that your L/C arrived late.

   不能否认你方信用证迟到。

7. in no case 决不，一点也不

   e.g. The shipment should, in no case, be made later than May.

   在任何情况下，装运都不应迟于5月。

8. step up 加速；促进

   e.g. To step up the trade, we are prepared to lower our price by 5%.

   为了加快贸易，我们准备把价格降低5%。

9. counter-offer [ˈkaʊntə(r) ˈɒfə(r)] v./n. 还盘

   e.g. The price you counter-offered is not in line with the prevailing market.

   你方还盘的价格与现行市场不符。

   e.g. If you cannot accept, please make best possible counter-offer.

   如果你不能接受，请尽可能地还盘。

10. on or before 在某日或某日之前；不迟于……，这个词组用于明确时间界限

11. decline [diˈklain] vt. 拒绝，谢绝 vi. 下降

    e.g. We are obliged to decline fresh order as we cannot expect new supplies to come in.

    我们不得不拒绝新订单，因为我们不能指望有新的供应。

e.g. For this reason, we cannot but decline your proposal.

因此,我们不得不拒绝你的建议。

e.g. Our buyers decline raising(or: to raise) their limit.

我们的买家拒绝提高他们的限额。

e.g. The market has declined in the last few weeks.

市场在过去几周已经下跌。

12. acceptance [əkˈseptəns] n. 接受

e.g. We strongly recommend your acceptance for our stocks are running low.

我们强烈建议你方接受,因为我们的存货正在减少。

(2) **Counter-offer on Price of Medical Apparatus and Instruments**

Dear Sirs,

We thank you for your Quotation No. 134 for your NVR-FM790 Medical Apparatus and Instruments, and we have given it very careful consideration.

We don't deny that we are interested in your products, as you know. However, we find that we can obtain from another firm a price of 5% lower than that of yours.

If you would reduce your price to that extent, we will be pleased to place with you an order that will carry us for the rest of this year.

Hope to hear from you soon.

Yours truly,

 Notes

1. medical apparatus and instruments 医疗器械
2. deny [diˈnai] v. 否认;否定;拒绝承认

   e.g. The government has denied that there was a plot to assassinate the president.

   政府否认曾有人密谋暗杀总统。

   e.g. I denied my father because I wanted to become someone else.

   我和父亲断绝了关系,因为我想成为一个不一样的自己。

3. to that extent 到那种程度

   e.g. To that extent, they are accidental.

在这种程度上说,它们的发生是具有偶然性的。

e.g. This had never been achieved to that extent before in computer animation.

在电脑动画中,从来没有人能够做到这种程度。

4. place with you an order 向你方订货

2. Declining a Counter-offer

（1）Declining a Counter-offer on Sewing Machines

Dear Sirs,

<u>Butterfly Sewing Machines</u>

We learn from your letter of April 18th that our price for the subject article is found to be on the high side.

Much as we would like to cooperate with you in expanding sales, we are regretful that we just cannot see our way clear to entertain your counter-offer, as the price we quoted is quite realistic. As a matter of fact, we have received a lot of orders from various sources at our level.

If you see any chance to do better, please let us know. Owing to a limited supply available at present, we would ask you to act quickly.

In the meantime, please keep us posted of developments at your end. We assure you that any further enquiries from you will receive our prompt attention.

Yours faithfully,

×××

 Notes

1. subject ['sʌbdʒikt, səb'dʒekt] n. 标题;主题

    e.g. We have read your letter of January 23rd on the above subject.

    关于上述主题,我们已阅读了你方1月23日的来函。

2. see one's way (clear) to 有可能(做某事);设法

    e.g. We hope you will see your way to accept October shipment.

我们希望你方能够接受10月份装运。

e.g. We feel regretful that we cannot see our way clear to accept payment terms other than L/C.

很遗憾我们不能接受信用证以外的付款方式。

3. realistic [ˌriːəˈlistik] adj. 符合实际的

   e.g. Your price is not quite realistic.

   你方价格不符合实际。

4. do better 出较高的(或更低的)价格

   e.g. If later on you can see any chance to do better, please let us know.

   如果以后你能出更高(或低)的价格,请告诉我们。

5. available [əˈveiləbl] adj. 可利用的;可得到的;可供应的

   e.g. We will ship your order by the first steamer available next month.

   我们将用下个月第一艘可定的轮船将您的订单装船。

   e.g. We regret to advise that we have no stock available at present.

   很遗憾,我们目前没有存货。

6. keep sb. posted (of) 随时告知某人 【同义】keep sb. informed/ advised (of)

   e.g. Please keep us posted of any change in situation.

   如果情况有任何变化,请随时通知我们。

7. development [diˈveləpmənt] n. 发展;进展

   e.g. We look forward to the rapid development of our business.

   我们期待业务的快速发展。

8. assure [əˈʃuə(r)] v. 保证;(使)确信

   e.g. We assure you of our readiness to cooperate with you.

   我们向您保证我们愿意与您合作。

   e.g. We assure you that we shall do our best to expedite shipment.

   我们向你方保证,我们将尽最大努力加速装运。

9. receive one's attention 得到注意;予以办理

   e.g. Your letter has received our careful attention.

   你的信受到了我们的仔细关注。

 (2) Declining Request for Price Reduction

Dear Sirs,

We regret very much having to decline your counter-offer of December 16th on "Tas" Brand Steel Door.

It's our usual practice to quote 5% above the cost. More important, the costs of raw materials have risen a lot since June and we have to adjust our prices upwards accordingly. But even with the increase, our prices are still lower if compared with those from other competitors in the same line.

The price may rise as a result of present large demand. We will keep the offer open for you until December 24th, after which date we can't ensure that the goods will still be available.

Please take the above into careful consideration and fax us your order immediately.

Yours faithfully,

 Notes

1. regret ［ri'gret］ *n./v.* 遗憾；抱歉

    e.g. Much to our regret, we are unable to help you in price.

    很抱歉,价格方面我们无法帮你。

    e.g. We regret to say that, after repeated efforts, we haven't yet found the goods you need.

    很抱歉,经过再三努力,我们还是没有找到你们需要的货物。

    e.g. They regret to find that the quality of the goods is not up to the agreed standard.

    他们遗憾地发现货物的质量与商定的标准不符。

    regretful ［ri'gretfl］ *adj.* 抱歉的；懊悔的

    e.g. We are very regretful that we don't have the items in stock at present.

    很抱歉,这些商品目前无货可供。

    regrettable ［ri'gretəbl］ *adj.* 令人遗憾的

    e.g. It is regrettable to learn that the business has fallen through.

    我们遗憾地获悉交易落空。

2. adjust ［ə'dʒʌst］ *v.* 调整；(使)适应

    e.g. They have adjusted their product structure to the changing world market.

    他们调整了产品结构以适应不断变化的世界市场。

    e.g. We must adjust to the bad economic situation.

    我们必须调整以适应恶劣的经济形势。

    adjustment ［ə'dʒʌstmənt］ *n.* 调整；适应

    e.g. The Chinese government will seriously consider adjustment of taxation policy in the capital market.

中国政府将会认真考虑有关资本市场税收政策的调整事宜。

e.g. Miss Linda made a quick adjustment to her new job.

琳达小姐迅速地调整自己以适应新工作。

3. accordingly [əˈkɔːdiŋli] adv. 因此(句首或句中)；相应地(句末)

e.g. Accordingly, the manufacturer will try to improve the quality of their products to take a bigger share of the market.

因此，制造商将努力提高产品的质量以争取更大的市场份额。

e.g. Please indicate the goods which can't be supplied to the specifications so that we can make arrangement accordingly.

请指出哪些商品无法按规格定制以便我们作相应的安排。

4. competitor [kəmˈpetitə(r)] n. 竞争者

e.g. Our goods are much better than those from our competitors in both quality and price.

我们的货物在质量和价格上比竞争对手的要好得多。

competition n. 竞争

e.g. With the sole agency in your hand, there will be no competition and you can easily control the market.

有了独家代理权，就会没有竞争，你们很容易控制市场。

compete [kəmˈpiːt] v. 竞争

e.g. They have to compete with a lot of suppliers for the Southeast Asian market.

他们要与很多供货商竞争东南亚市场。

competitive [kəmˈpetətiv] adj. 竞争的；有竞争力的

e.g. Our offer is competitive and we cannot lower the price any more.

我方的报价是有竞争力的，我们不能再降价了。

3. Acceptance of a Counter-offer

（1）Acceptance of a Counter-offer on Women's Shirts

Dear Sirs,

Your letter of May 13th asking us to reduce our quotation for 40,000 pieces of women's shirts by 9% has been received by us today.

We feel it very regrettable that you find our price on the high side. As stated in our previous letter, our goods are well received in many countries because of their fine quality and reasonable price. All our prices have been carefully calculated and cut to the limit, at which we have done large business with many other buyers in different countries.

However, in order to encourage your business with us, we are prepared to meet you half way by making a further reduction of 4% in our quotation. This is the best we can do and we hope it will be acceptable to you.

We are looking forward to receiving your orders at an early date.

Yours faithfully,

×××

 Notes

1. acceptance [əkˈseptəns] *n.* 接受

    e.g. Unless we have your acceptance before the end of this week, we will have to put the offer out.

    除非你方在本周末前接受，否则我们将不得不结束此发盘。

    accept [əkˈsept] *vt./vi.* 接受（报盘、订单等）

    e.g. They refused to accept our request for price reduction without giving any reasons.

    他们没有给出任何理由拒绝接受我们的降价要求。

    e.g. This is our bottom price. Please accept as early as you can if it satisfies you.

    这是我们的底价。如果您满意，请尽早接受。

    acceptable [əkˈseptəbl] *adj.* 可以接受的

    e.g. Should the design and workmanship be acceptable to our customers, large orders will follow.

    如果设计和工艺能为我们的客户所接受，我们将大量订购。

    e.g. If you compare our price with that of others, you will find it acceptable.

    如果你把我方价格和其他价格比较一下，你会发现它是可以接受的。

2. on the high side （价格等）偏高　　on the low side （价格等）偏低

    e.g. It seems that your price is on the high side, which prohibits us from placing an order with you.

    你方价格似乎偏高，因此我们无法向你方订货。

    e.g. As your price is rather on the high side, we regret our inability to place orders with you.

    由于你方价格偏高，我们很遗憾不能向你方订货。

    e.g. We regret being unable to accept your bid as it is on the low side.

我们很遗憾不能接受你方的报价,因为它价格偏低。

3. be well received 畅销,受欢迎 【同义】enjoy fast /excellent sales; be popular with sb.; sell fast/well; command a good market/sale

   e.g. Our garments are well received in the world market because of their attractive designs.

   我们的服装因其吸引人的设计而在世界市场上广受欢迎。

4. cut [kʌt] vt. 削减(价格等);降低

   e.g. We are making every effort to cut expenses and avoid waste.

   我们正在尽一切努力减少开支,避免浪费。

   e.g. With its entry into the WTO, China will cut considerably the duties it imposes on the goods from other member countries.

   加入世贸组织后,中国将大幅削减对其他成员国货物征收的关税。

5. meet sb. half way 各让一半

   e.g. In view of your business amount, we would agree to meet you half way.

   考虑到你方的业务量,我们同意各让一半。

   e.g. After repeated efforts, they agreed to meet each other half way.

   经过多次努力,他们同意各让一半。

6. further ['fɜːðə(r)] adj. 更多的;另外的 adv. 进一步地;继续地

   e.g. It's a pity that you are unable to make a further reduction in your price.

   很遗憾你方不能再进一步降价了。

   e.g. We look forward to your further orders.

   我们期待着您的进一步订单。

   e.g. We hope to promote, by joint efforts, our mutually beneficial business relations further.

   我们希望通过共同努力,进一步促进我们互利的业务关系。

7. at an early date 早日,尽早

   e.g. Kindly let us have your specific enquiry at an early date.

   请早日告知具体询盘。

   e.g. We would like you to quote us at an early date, stating individual price of each model.

   我们希望你们早日给我们报价,并说明每种型号的价格。

(2) Acceptance of a Counter-offer on Tools

Dear Mr. Chen,

We thank you for your letter of February 22nd, 2019 giving us a counter-offer for 1,000 sets of tools.

Although your price is below our level, we have finally decided to accept your counter-offer of USD 3.50 per set CIF Guangzhou with a view to initiating our business with you at an early date.

In addition, we would like to make the following details for your confirmation:
Packing: in cartons
Insurance: to be covered by the seller for 105% of the invoice value against All Risks & War Risk.

We are waiting for your confirmation by return.

Sincerely yours,

×××

Notes

1. CIF(Cost Insurance and Freight) 到岸价格(成本加保险费、运费)

    e.g. By CIF invoice, the price includes all the expenses of cost, freight and insurance.
    CIF发票包括所有的成本、运输和保险的款项。

2. with a view to 为了；以便

    e.g. The current political situation was considered with a view to its causes and its effect.
    从原因和后果两个方面对时局进行了考虑。

    e.g. The authors no doubt overstated their case with a view to catching the public's attention.
    这些作者无疑夸大了实情以吸引公众的注意力。

3. initiate [iˈniʃieit, iˈniʃiət] v. 开始；着手

    e.g. They wanted to initiate a discussion on economics.
    他们想启动一次经济学讨论。

    e.g. The trip was initiated by the manager of the community centre.
    这次旅行由社区活动中心的经理发起。

    initial adj. 首次的，初期的

    e.g. The aim of this initial meeting is to clarify the issues.
    本次初步会议的目标是澄清这些问题。

    e.g. I'm also not crazy about the initial terms of the deal.
    我对该协议的最初条款也不太满意。

4. in carton 用纸箱装

5. to be covered by the seller for 105% of the invoice value against All Risks & War Risk. 由卖方按发票金额的105%投保一切险和战争险

4. Partial Rejection

（1）**Partial Rejection of an Order**

Dear Sirs,

We have received your order of March 5th for a minimum quantity of 150 metric tons of Zinc Oxide 99.8%.

Had you contacted us earlier we could have complied with your request to the full. But now, with our stock appreciably diminished, the maximum we can supply is 100 tons. The remainder can be replaced by Zinc Oxide 99.5%, which is a new type almost similar to 99.8% but priced lower by 3%. Of course, this substitution is subject to your approval. If you agree to our proposal, it is a deal; otherwise, you would have to be satisfied with only 100 tons for the time being.

For your prompt attention, we have sent you an email this morning to the above effect.

Yours faithfully,

×××

 Notes

1. minimum ['miniməm] *n.* 最小量,最低额 *adj.* 最小的,最低的

    e.g. The price is their minimum; they refuse to lower it any further.
    这是他们的最低价,他们拒绝再降价。

    e.g. Fifty tons is the minimum quantity they will take.
    50吨是他们所要的最低数量。

2. to the full 完全地

    e.g. We are glad that we can supply your needs to the full.
    我们很高兴能充分满足您的需求。

3. appreciably [ə'priːʃəbli] *adv.* 可感到地,可看见地;明显地

e.g. The price has advanced appreciably.

价格已明显上涨。

e.g. The pound has appreciably lowered in value.

英镑已明显贬值。

4. diminish [di'miniʃ] vt. (使)减少 vi. 减少

e.g. Owing to heavy bookings, our stocks have diminished to a large extent.

由于大量的预订,我们的库存在很大程度上减少了。

5. maximum ['mæksiməm] n. 最大量,最高额 adj. 最大的,最高的【反义】minimum

e.g. 5% commission is the maximum we allow for articles of this kind.

5%的佣金是我们对这种商品的最高限额。

e.g. We understand quite well that you have stretched your efforts to the maximum extent.

我们很清楚你已经尽了最大努力了。

6. remainder [ri'meində(r)] n. 剩余;遗留

e.g. What about the remainder of the order?

剩下的订单呢?

7. replace [ri'pleis] v. 代替

e.g. We agree to replace Item No. 25 with No. 30.

我方同意将第25项替换为第30项。

e.g. Item No. 25 will be replaced by No. 30.

第25项将替换为第30项。

8. price [prais] v. 开价,定价

e.g. Please price your offer as low as possible.

请把你的报价定得尽可能低。

9. approval [ə'pru:vl] n. 赞成;认可

e.g. This new product of ours has met with wide approval.

我们的这种新产品得到了广泛认可。

10. deal [di:l] n. 交易

e.g. We have closed several big deals with them.

我们已经和他们达成了几笔大交易。

11. otherwise ['ʌðəwaiz] adv. 不同地,在不同方面;在其他方面 conj. 否则

e.g. Our future offers will include your 2% commission unless otherwise advised.

除非另有通知,否则我们今后的报价将包括你方2%的佣金。

e.g. The admixture is a little too high, but otherwise the shipment is satisfactory.

掺合料有点太高,但除此之外,装运是令人满意的。

e.g. Please rush your L/C otherwise shipment will be delayed.

请加急信用证,否则装船将延误。

12. to the above effect 按以上的意思

（2）**Partial Rejection on Payment Terms**

Dear Sirs,

We thank you for your quotation of January 4th for 500 sets of Panasonic 3166 Colour TV. We find your price as well as delivery date satisfactory, however we would give our suggestion of an alteration of your payment terms.

Our past purchase of other household electrical appliances from you has been paid as a rule by confirmed, irrevocable letter of credit at sight. On this basis, it has indeed cost us a great deal. From the moment to open credit till the time our buyers pay us, the tie-up of our funds lasts about four months. Under the present circumstances, this question is particularly taxing owing to the tight money condition and unprecedentedly high bank interest.

In view of our long business relations and our amicable cooperation prospects, we suggest that you accept either "Cash against Documents on arrival of goods" or "Drawing on us at 60 days sight".

Your first priority to the consideration of the above request and an early favourable reply will be highly appreciated.

Yours faithfully,

×××

 Notes

1. alteration [ˌɔːltəˈreɪʃn] *n*. 改变,改动
2. household electrical appliances 家用电器
3. as a rule 通常 【同义】usually
   e.g. As a rule, we give our agents 3% commission.
   通常我们给代理商3%的佣金。
4. taxing [ˈtæksɪŋ] *adj*. 难以负担的;使人感到有压力的
   e.g. Such an amount is taxing for a firm of moderate means.
   这样一笔数额对一个中等财力的商号来说是有压力的。
5. tie-up of funds 占用资金

tight *adj.*（钱，商品等）紧的；难得到的

tight money 银根紧俏

6. unprecedentedly [ʌnˈpresidentidli] *adv.* 空前地

   e.g. As a result of energy crisis, the price of oil is unprecedentedly high.

   由于能源危机，石油价格空前高涨。

7. cash against documents on arrival of goods 货到后凭单付款，简称 CAD (Cash Against Documents)

8. drawing on us at 60 days sight 开出见票60天付款的汇票向我们收款

   draw *v.* 开出（汇票），指开立票据时，及物动词 draw 作"开立"解，不及物动词 draw 作"开立票据"解，因此，draw(*vt.*) a draft ＝ draw(*vi.*)

   draw (a draft) on sb. for ... 开出向某人索取……的汇票

   e.g. As agreed, we are drawing (a draft) on you for the value of this sample shipment.

   按照商定，对这批样货的价款，我们开出汇票向你方索取。

   draw on sb. against sth. 开出汇票向某人索取某笔款项

   e.g. As agreed, we are drawing on you at sight against your purchase of a sample lot.

   按照商定，对你方所购样货我们开出即期汇票向你方索款。

   drawings *n.*(*pl.*) 用汇票支取的金额

   e.g. Your letter of credit is to allow 5% more or less in drawings.

   你方信用证应准许在收款时有5%的上下浮动。

9. priority [praiˈɒrəti] *n.* 优先

   top priority 最优先考虑的事

   first priority 最优先考虑的事

   give priority to 给……以优先权；优先考虑……

   e.g. We will give (first or top) priority to your orders.

   我们对你方的订单将给予最优先考虑。

   take (top or first) priority in 在……中占优先地位

   e.g. The question of payment will take top priority in our discussions.

   支付问题将在我们讨论中占最优先地位。

   enjoy priority in 在……方面享有优先权

   e.g. You may enjoy priority in our offers.

   你方可在我方报盘方面享有优先权。

Part Ⅳ Useful Expressions and Sentences

Expressions

1. make (sb.) a counter-offer (as follows)（向某人）还盘（如下）

2. (price) on the high/ low side （价格）偏高/低

3. be in (out of) line with the market 与市场(不)一致
   keep with the current market 与现行市场一致

4. at a price ...% lower than ... 价格比……低……%

5. meet sb. halfway 各让一半；折中处理

6. make any further reduction 再次降价，作进一步的降价

7. (price) fixed at a reasonable level 定价合理

8. market is weak；market is declining 市场疲软；市场正在下滑

9. maximum quantity 最大数量
   minimum quantity 最小数量

10. (the price) has advanced ...%/ considerably （价格）已上涨……%/明显上涨

Typical Sentences

1. Thank you for your prompt reply and detailed quotation.

2. Much to our regret，we cannot entertain business at your price，since it is out of line with the prevailing market，being 20% lower than the average.

3. We are sorry to tell you that we cannot take you up on the offer since the price you are asking is above the market level here for the quality in question.

4. In view of our long-standing business relationship we make you the following counter-offer.

5. Your competitors are offering considerably lower prices and unless you can reduce your quotations，we shall have to buy elsewhere.

6. We hope that you will take our counter-offer seriously into consideration and reply very soon.

7. We hope you will consider our counter-offer most favorably and fax us your acceptance as soon as possible.

8. It is impossible for us to entertain your counter-offer.

9. This is our rock-bottom price. We can't make any further reduction.

10. We appreciate your counter-offer but find it too low to accept.

Part V Practical Training

I. Elementary Training

1. Choose the best answer.

(1) We are sorry we cannot ____ your counter-offer. Your bid is much too low.
   A. entertain   B. agree   C. consider   D. receive

(2) We would therefore suggest ____ your own interest that you send your acceptance as soon as possible.
   A. for   B. to   C. in   D. at

(3) Your offer is out of line ____ the price ____ in the present market.
   A. in, acceptable   B. with, ruling
   C. at, being ruled   D. in, ruling

(4) We suggest that you ____ our offer immediately.
   A. will accept   B. accept   C. will consider   D. consider

(5) We regret that there is no stipulation of transshipment ____ allowed in your L/C.
   A. is   B. has been   C. being   D. are

(6) We believe we can ____ the users to divert their purchases to Korean products.
   A. convince   B. say   C. persuade   D. inform

(7) Material of similar products is easily obtainable ____ a much lower level.
   A. at   B. on   C. from   D. for

(8) We ____ allow you a 3% quantity discount if your order exceeds 2,000 dozen.
   A. are prepared   B. are prepared to
   C. will be prepared   D. will prepare

(9) Previous ____ the signing of the contract, there had been fierce arguments.
   A. to   B. on   C. by   D. in

(10) As we have cut our price to USD 20 per doz., we regret being unable to accept your request ____ further reduction.
   A. with   B. in   C. for   D. to

(11) We need all the necessary ____ regarding your products ____ now.
   A. information, exporting   B. informations, exported
   C. information. exported   D. information, for export

(12) Only ____ reducing the price by 6% ____ come to business.

  A. by, we can B. in, we can C. on, can we D. by, can we

(13) We are in receipt of your letter dated January 8th, ____ we are pleased to learn that you want to order 100 tons of the subject goods.

  A. in which B. from which C. to which D. at which

(14) The buyers ____ the sellers to ship the canned fruits within a month.

  A. demand B. demand to C. demanded of D. have demanded

(15) In your letter of April 10th, you did not mention ____ the price of arts & crafts.

  A. to raise B. having raised C. rise D. having risen

2. Read the following letters and fill in each blank with prepositions.

Letter 1

Dear Sirs,

We are in possession of your letter dated July 5th, 2019 offering us Jinling Brand automatic washing machine at USD 120 per set FOB Guangzhou inclusive __(1)__ our 5% commission.

While appreciating the quality of your lines, we made a careful study of your offer. We find that your prices are too high to be acceptable. In fact, some suppliers are actually lowering their prices to push sales in the past three months. In order to make your product more competitive __(2)__ our market, we suggest that you reduce prices __(3)__ 10%. If you agree to our counter-suggestion, regular orders __(4)__ large numbers will be placed. Otherwise, we would have to place our order elsewhere.

Please let us have your email confirmation __(5)__ your earliest convenience.

                    Yours sincerely,

                    ×××

Letter 2

Dear Sirs,

        Re: chinaware

We have noted your fax (1) October 10th, 2019, regarding the captioned goods and regret that our offer has not been accepted.

We have to point out that your counter-offer is obviously (2) the low side. The price we offered is entirely (3) line (4) the market level and has been accepted by many other customers.

However, we now agree (5) your interest to renew our offer till the end of this month and recommend that you fax us your confirmation without delay.

Yours faithfully,

×××

3. **Translate the following English into Chinese.**

(1) to make a counter-offer as follows

(2) this price leaves us with only a small profit

(3) a price 5% lower than previous quotation

(4) the price fixed at a reasonable level

(5) the price has advanced considerably

(6) be not in a position to make any further reduction

(7) entertain business at a most competitive price

(8) (products) too highly priced

(9) out of line with

(10) considerable quantity

(11) In order to conclude the transaction, we are prepared to reduce the price to 30 pounds.

(12) Let's meet each other halfway and reduce the price by 2%.

(13) There has been a slump in price recently. We believe we'll have a hard time convincing our clients at your price.

(14) We regret that we can't see our way clear to accept your counter-offer as your price is on the high side.

(15) As is well known, some suppliers are actually lowering their prices to push sales.

(16) If it were not for the friendship between us, we would not have made a firm offer at such a low price.

(17) As the market is weak at present, your quotation is unworkable.

(18) Our price has been narrowly calculated and it is impossible to make any further reduction.

(19) Owing to heavy bookings, we cannot accept fresh orders at present.

(20) Owing to a shortage of stock, we regret that we are unable to accept your repeat order.

Ⅱ. Intermediate Training

1. Supply the missing words in the blanks of the following letter. The first letters are given.

Dear Madam or Sir,

Thank you for your o____ of February 20th, 2019 and the Teddy Bear sample you kindly sent us.

In reply, we r____ to say that we cannot accept your offer at your p____. You may be aware that some products of Indian origin have been s____ here at a l____ about 10% lower than yours. We do think that the quality of your products is better, but the d____ in price should not be so big. Meanwhile, the current market is also weak. To conclude this t____, we make a c____ as follows: Teddy Bears as the s____ sent to us on February 20th, 2019, US$ 8 per piece CIF London, other terms and conditions as per your letter of February 20th, 2019.

We await your early a____ .

Yours faithfully,

× × ×

2. Cloze. Choose the most suitable words form the list of words to fill in the blanks. Each word can be used only once.

| based | declining | reduce | keen | business | convincing |
| favourably | offering | ignored | long-standing |

Dear Mr. Cai,

Thank you for your letter of the 20th inst. __(1)__ us 5,000 kilos of Walnut meat at $ 5 per kilogram.

We are interested in your product but regret to say that we find your price rather high. We believe that we would have a hard time __(2)__ our clients at your price. There is also __(3)__ competition from suppliers in South Korea and Thailand. That cannot be __(4)__. Should you be ready to __(5)__ your price by 5%, we might come to a __(6)__ agreement.

We are making this counter-offer __(7)__ on the __(8)__ business relationship between us. As the market is __(9)__, we hope you will consider our counter-offer most __(10)__ and cable us as soon as possible.

Yours sincerely,

 3. Translate the following Chinese into English.

(1) 价格偏高/低

(2) 现行价格

(3) 价格飞涨

(4) 价格在持续下降

(5) 给折扣

(6) 各让一半,折中处理

(7) 长期的业务关系

(8) 定价合理

(9) 市场疲弱;市场正在下滑

(10) 最大数量;最小数量

(11) 贵方还盘与现行国际市场不一致。

(12) 这确实已经是我们的底价,恐怕我们不可能再做任何让步了。

(13) 很遗憾,你方所报价格太高,交易无法进行。

(14) 很遗憾我们无法接受你方 2019 年 5 月 10 日的还盘。

(15) 鉴于我们之间长期的贸易关系,特向你方做如下还盘。

(16) 我们的价格定位在比较适中的水平,按这种价格我们已经收到了大量订单。

(17) 我们所报的价格是非常具有竞争性的。不过如果你们的订单超过 10,000 件,我们可以提供10％的折扣。

(18) 按你们所报价格我们将无利可图。我们最多只能让价5％。

(19) 你们竞争对手的报价要低很多。除非你们降价,否则我们得从他处购买。

(20) 希望你方对我们的还盘给予认真的考虑并很快地答复我方。

Ⅲ. Advanced Traning

 1. Translate the following letter into English.

敬启者:

手绣丝围巾

感谢贵方9月3日传真所发标题下货物5,000件的报盘,每件价格为汉堡成本、保险费加运费在内价9.50英镑。

我方立即与客户取得联系,他们对贵方产品的质量和设计表现出了极大的兴趣。然而,他们认为贵方价格偏高,比平均价高出10％。他们表示,若贵方每件价格降到8.50英镑,将再增加1,000件的订货。因此,如果能满足他们的要求,这将是达成一大笔交易的有利时机。我方希望贵方能利用此机会并从不断扩大的市场中获益。

期盼贵方有利的答复。

谨上

2. On behalf of the addresser, compose a letter according to the given information and message. Remember to arrange the necessary parts in proper form as they should be set out in a business letter.

Information:

Sender's name: H. J. Wilkinson & Co. Ltd. (importer)

Sender's address: 245 Lombart Street, Lagos, Nigeria

Sender's cable address: 5527GFTDC

Sender's telex: 44388 GFTDC NG

Sender's fax number: 86-20-83328156

Date: September 18, 2019

Receiver's name: Guangdong Foreign Trade Development Corp. (exporter)

Receiver's address: 779 East Dongfeng Road, Guangzhou, China

Message:

告诉对方你已经收到2019年9月13日关于50,000件儿童踏板车的报盘信。

明确表示很遗憾无法接受,因为对方报价过高。并说明自去年12月以来,类似商品价格下跌了15％,一些供货商对超过50,000美元的订单甚至给予高达20％的特殊折扣。

因此，对于对方 FOB 广州每件 18.5 美元的价格很难接受。除非对方降价 10%，否则我方将别无选择，只得向别处报盘。

鉴于双方之间有着长期良好业务关系才作出此还盘，建议对方重新考虑并立即接受该还盘。

Module 3
Conclusion of Business
交易的达成

Unit 5 Order and Contract
订单与合同

Lead-in

Try to finish the following tasks and predict the objectives of this unit.

Task 1

假设你是广东服装进出口公司的业务员。最近你收到英国一家公司发来的有关订购女士衬衫的订单。你公司愿意按照订单上所列的价格供应该货物,请代表公司以订单的形式拟一份确认函,信中务必包含以下内容。

(1) 贵公司关于 6,000 件女士衬衫的订单已收到,谢谢!

(2) 我们确认按贵方来函中所提条件成交的女士衬衫订单如下:

货号	数量	单价	总价
5-001	2,000 件	30 美元/件	60,000 美元
5-002	3,000 件	20 美元/件	60,000 美元
5-003	1,000 件	40 美元/件	40,000 美元
总计			160,000 美元

(所有价格均为成本加保险费、运费至纽约)

(3) 其他条件与贵方来函中所提内容一致。

(4) 我方保证按时按质履行订单,请贵公司务必及时开证以免耽误装运。

(5) 除你们所订几款样式外,我公司还经营其他样式的女士长裙。随附目录单和价格表,如有需要,请联系我们。

Task 2

假设你是上海进出口公司的经理。最近,你收到美国一家贸易公司发来的关于红茶的

订单。现在请代表公司拟函确认该订单,并附上拟好的合同要求对方会签。请注意信中务必包含以下内容:

(1) 我们很高兴确认贵方订购红茶的第553号订单。

(2) 随函附寄我方第B-32号合同一式两份,请查收并会签,并尽快寄回一份以供我方存档。

(3) 期盼早日收到会签的合同。

Part Ⅰ Introduction

1. 订单

订单指买家购买商品的发盘,这个协议只有经卖家确认才有约束力。此后,买卖双方必须遵守这个协议。因此在你写订单时,一定要将主要的交易条件描述清楚、准确。

订单可以通过函电、传真、电子邮件等方式发出。当卖家收到订单后,应该对订单立即确认。如果所定的货物不能立即提供或者发货,应该回信告知对方原因。

2. 合同

在接受实盘或确认接受后,一般由卖方制定合同或者是销售确认书,然后买卖双方签字。销售合同或者销售确认书一经签字即刻生效。

合同或者销售确认书必须包含所有谈判过程中商定的细节,合同还包含比如检验、索赔、仲裁和不可抗力等惯例条款。一旦发生争议,这是唯一一个作为判断依据的官方文件。

Part Ⅱ Letter Writing Guide

1. For letters concerning orders 订单信

When writing an order letter, you must include all the specifics necessary to complete the order to your satisfaction. To make your order clear and easy to understand, you should use the listing format of the order form as a guide to give information about the following matters:

(1) a full description of the commodity, including model, number, size, color, or any other relevant information

(2) quantity

(3) date and method of shipment

(4) price per item

(5) packing

(6) payment

2. For letters concerning contracts 寄送合同信

In a letter sending or making mention of a contract, the following contents should be included.

(1) confirming the business agreement

(2) stating that you have enclosed an order form/ contract/ sales confirmation

(3) requesting the return expectation of the counter-signature, promising or hoping that the contract would be fulfilled smoothly and successfully, and that the mutual business would be expanded in the future

Part Ⅲ   Sample Letters

1. Placing an Order

Dear Sirs,

From the samples you sent us in April, we have made selections and have the pleasure of giving you the following order on usual terms for shipment to Sydney:

Quantity	Items	Catalogue Number	Price
150 cartons	Health Tea	T16	US$ 110 per carton
250 cartons	Wen Jing Tea	T17	US$ 120 per carton
350 cartons	Fat Reducing Tea	T18	US$ 130 per carton

For your information, we have applied for the import license and the letter of credit for this order. Since we need the goods urgently, you are requested to effect shipment one month after receipt of our L/C. There is a good market for the said items and, if this initial order is satisfactorily executed, we are prepared to place repeat orders with you in the near future.

We are awaiting your confirmation and prompt delivery.

Yours faithfully,

×××

Notes

1. effect shipment 装船,装运【同义】make (arrange, expedite) shipment
2. said [sed] *adj.* 所说的,所提及的(以避免重复前面出现的事物或者名称)【同义】mentioned before (above)
3. after receipt of 收到……后

    e.g. Generally, shipment can be effected within 30 days after receipt of your official order.

    一般来说,接到你方正式订单30天内装运。

2. Confirming an Order

Dear Sirs,

Re: video camera recorder

Further to our recent discussions through fax and email, we should like to confirm details of ordering the above mentioned goods:

Quantity	Description	Unit Price	Amount
500 pieces	NV-FJ630	USD 120.00	USD 60,000.00

The above price is on CFR Guangzhou basis.

Packing: Each piece is packed in a polybag then in a carton.

Payment: By irrevocable documentary letter of credit opened with Bank of China and drawn at sight.

Delivery: As we need the goods urgently, please deliver within 40 days after receipt of the order.

We would like you to send us your acknowledgement of this order at your earliest convenience. When we receive your acknowledgement we will arrange to apply for L/C.

Your early attention to this order will be highly appreciated.

Your faithfully,

×××

Notes

1. video camera recorder 摄录机
2. description [diˈskripʃn] n. 规格
3. carton [ˈkɑːtn] n. 纸箱
4. irrevocable documentary letter of credit opened with Bank of China and drawn at sight 由中国银行开立的不可撤销跟单即期信用证

3. Acceptance of an Order

Dear Sirs,

We highly appreciate your Order No. 8803 for 400 sets of Double Happiness Brand Automatic Washing Machines and are pleased to confirm that the goods can be supplied from stock. We are confident that you will be satisfied with the quality of our goods.

As for method of payment, we quite agree with you that you establish a confirmed, irrevocable L/C for a sum not exceeding US$ 72,000 and valid till August 10th. Upon receipt of confirmation of the L/C from the National Bank, your order will be ready for shipment to await your agent's shipping instructions.

We hope that the goods will reach you in good time and that we may have further orders from you.

Yours faithfully,

×××

 Notes

1. automatic washing machines 全自动洗衣机
2. shipping instructions 装船指示
3. ... can be supplied from stock 现货供应
4. upon receipt of 一收到……就……
5. in good time 及时【同义】in time

   e.g. We can ensure you regular supplies of these materials if you pay for them in good time.
   如果你们能按时付款,我们可以保证定期向你们供应这些材料。

4. Rejecting an Order

Dear Sirs,

We refer to your Order No. FR246 and regret to say that we are not able to accept your bid price for Frozen Rabbit Meat.

As you may be aware that the prices for foodstuffs have gone up sharply owing to the rough weather, it is impossible to purchase supplies at economic prices. Moreover, we have improved our packing method, as you may have seen from our samples, which cost us a lot. The price, therefore, is 8% higher than your bid.

As the market is firm with an upward tendency, we advise you to accept our piece without delay. In view of our long business connection we will definitely keep supplies available for you if you amend the price in your order within 5 days.

Yours faithfully,

×××

 Notes

1. refer to 谈及

    e.g. We refer to your offer No. PL520 for 3,000 drums of petroleum.

    兹谈及你方关于3,000桶石油的PL520号报盘。

2. bid [bid] *vt./n.* 报价；投标

    bid price 递价；买方报价

3. rough weather 狂风暴雨的天气

4. at economic prices 经济的价格；较低的价格

5. the market is firm with an upward tendency 市场坚挺有上涨趋势

    with an upward tendency 上涨趋势

    with a downward tendency 下降趋势

5. Enclosing a Contract

Dear Mr. Huang,

Referring to the faxes exchanged between us resulting in the conclusion of business for 200 tons of Oysters, we are enclosing our S/C Number 39 in duplicate. Please countersign and return the bottom copy to us for our files.

We trust you will open the necessary letter of credit as soon as possible.

Your quick answer will be appreciated.

Sincerely yours,

×××

 Notes

1. Oyster ['ɔistər] n. 牡蛎
2. S/C (Sales Confirmation) 销售确认书,也可以认作是销售合同。两者并无本质区别,都是买卖双方签订的书面销售协议,若其中对双方的某些商务行为都作了法律后果的界定,就都可以作为日后循法律途径解决争议和纠纷的依据之一。
3. duplicate ['dju:plikeit] n. 完全一样的东西;复制品;副本 adj. 完全一样的;复制的;副本的

   in duplicate 一式两份
4. bottom copy 副本

6. Enclosing a Counter-signed Contract

Dear Mr. Sims,

Thank you very much for your letter of July 28th, 2019 concerning the Sales Contract Number 39.

We have checked the entire contract and are satisfied with it. Enclosed please find one signed copy for your file.

We have applied for the L/C through our bank in your favor covering the said products and would be grateful if you can execute the order as quickly as possible.

We are looking forward to your reply.

Sincerely yours

×××

Notes

1. applied for L/C though ... bank 通过……银行开立信用证
2. the said ... 所说的……，所述的……
3. execute the order 执行该订单

Part Ⅳ Useful Expressions and Sentences

Expressions

1. fresh/ new order 新订单　　　　　initial order 首次订单
   outstanding order 未完成订单　　　trial order 试订单
   duplicate order 续订单　　　　　　repeat orders 重复订单
   amended order 修改后的订单
2. accept an ordcr 接受订单　book an order 订货　confirm an order 确认订单
3. cancel an order 取消订单　withdraw an order 撤消订单
4. carry out/ work on/ execute/ fill/ fulfill an order 执行订单
5. decline/ refuse/ turn down an order 拒绝订单
6. send (give) sb. an order for sth. = place an order with sb. for sth. 向某人下订单订购……
7. order sth. at ... (price) 以……价格订购某物
8. confirm acceptance of one's order 确认接受某人订单
9. ensure the fulfillment of an order 保证订单的执行
10. draw up/ draft a contract 草拟/起草合同　to have a contract ready for signature 备好合同签字
11. to enter into/ sign/ close a contract 签订合同
12. sign/ countersign and return a copy of ... for one's file/record 签/会签并退一份

……供某人存档/备案
13. counter-signature 会签,联署
14. in duplicate/ triplicate/ quadruplicate/ quintuplicate/ sextuplicate/ septuplicate/ octuplicate/ nonuplicate/ decuplicate 一式二/三/四/五/六/七/八/九/十份

Typical Sentences

Sentences Concerning Orders

1. We have the pleasure of sending you an order for 1,000 dozen umbrellas, at US$ 45 per dozen CIF New York, based on your catalog No. 51 of July 1st.

2. We shall place a large order with you provided the quantity of the goods and shipping period meet our requirement.

3. We are pleased to find that your material appears to be of fine quality. As a trial, we are delighted to send you a small order for 2,500 dozen rubber shoes.

4. We have pleasure in informing you that we have accepted your order No. 234 for 120 units of Italian furniture Number TS-11 at $ 320 per unit FOB Genoa as follows.

5. To our regret, we are unable to accept your order for 500 pieces of pillowcases at the price requested, since our profit margin does not allow us any concession to discount the price.

6. As wages and prices of materials have risen considerably, we regret that we are not in a position to book the order for 500 cases canned beef at the prices we quoted half a year ago.

7. We have received your order. It is booked and we are processing it. As the T-shirts you ordered are now in stock, we will ship them without fail as early as possible.

8. If you do not have the quality JS208 in stock, we shall have to cancel this order, as we are not interested in any substitute.

9. We have seen the samples and are sending you a trial order for 50,000 toys of the following particulars. We sincerely hope that the order will be punctually fulfilled.

10. We have received your Order Number 751 and it will be executed to your satisfaction.

11. We place this order on the understanding that the consignment is dispatched by September 15th and that we reserve the right to cancel it and to refuse delivery after the date.

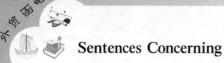

Sentences Concerning Contracts

1. We are sending you our Sales Confirmation Number 789 in duplicate. Please sign and return one copy for our file.
2. Thank you for your letter of April 8th, and the enclosed order sheet for 1,000 sets of sewing machines. We are enclosing our S/C No. 345 in duplicate, please countersign and return one copy to us for our file.
3. Enclosed is our Sales Contract No. 986 in duplicate. If you find everything in order, please sign and return one copy for our record.
4. As a result of the recent exchange of cables between us, we confirm having booked your Order No.369 on the terms and conditions set forth in the enclosed S/C No.939, in duplicate. Please counter-sign one copy and return to us for our file.
5. We are pleased to enclose our Contract No. 589 in two originals. Please counter-sign one of the originals and return to us for our records.
6. Enclosed please find our Sales Confirmation Number 996 in duplicate for your counter-signature. Please sign and return one copy to us for our records as soon as possible.
7. Please send the duplicate of the contract countersigned to us.

Part Ⅴ Practical Training

Ⅰ. Elementary Training

1. Choose the best answer.

(1) We are prepared to inform you ____ your order will be ready ____ dispatch next month.

    A. that; for   B. that; to   C. of; in   D. of; for

(2) It is necessary that the specifications ____ the requirements.

    A. confirm to   B. conform to   C. confirm with   D. conform

(3) These are the only terms ____ we can do business.

    A. on what   B. in what   C. on which   D. in which

(4) We are prepared to give you this special accommodation with the view ____ encouraging further business.

A. in B. for C. on D. of

(5) We price this new product economically with a view ____ promoting the transaction.

A. to B. for C. in D. on

(6) We shall appreciate it very much if you will give us indication ____ you think you could conclude business.

A. to which B. at which C. in that D. on that

(7) ____ our S/C No. 44 in duplicate for your signature and please return one copy for our file.

A. Enclose please find B. We are enclosed
C. We enclose D. Enclosing please find

(8) If the ABC Co. can renew the offer for further five days, we think we shall be able to put ____ the business.

A. through B. on C. into D. forward

(9) We are pleased to confirm ____ with you the transaction of 3,000 metric tons soybean.

A. having concluded B. to have concluded
C. have come to terms D. to have carried out

(10) We confirm our sale of the following commodities ____ terms and conditions ____ set forth below.

A. in; that B. on; which C. for; as D. on; as

2. Read the following letters and fill in each black with prepositions.

Letter 1

Dear Mr. Chen,

Thank you for your letter of September 21st 2019 __(1)__ which you enclosed your price list and catalogue.

As we find both quality and prices satisfactory, we are pleased to give you a trial order __(2)__ the following items __(3)__ the understanding from stock __(4)__ the price named.

... (order form)

Since our customers urgently require all these items, we hope you will make delivery __(5)__ an early date.

Your quick answer would be appreciated.

                Sincerely yours,

                × × ×

Letter 2

Dear Mr. Snyder,

We refer __(1)__ your fax of July 30th, 2019 regarding the repeat order __(2)__ Garment.

We regret that we are unable to fill your order, as our manufactures are heavily committed(任务满了).

We will, however, keep your order and as soon as we are __(3)__ a position to accept new orders we will contact you by fax.

__(4)__ regard to stock lines, we are enclosing a list __(5)__ your information. Should you be interested in any items, please inform us of your requirements.

                Sincerely yours,

                × × ×

3. Translate the following English into Chinese.

 (1) on usual terms

 (2) effect shipment

 (3) a good market for ...

 (4) with regard to

 (5) additional orders

 (6) prompt shipment

 (7) confirm an order

(8) shipping instructions

(9) initial order

(10) placing an order

(11) We are hereby pleased to place an order for 100 sets of sewing machines with you, at USD 250 each set.

(12) We enclose a trial order as the quality is up to our expectation. We will send duplicate orders in the near future.

(13) With reference to your letter of September 5th 2019, we have pleasure in informing you that we have booked your order for 2,000 sets of clocks.

(14) Thank you for your letter of April 8th and the enclosed order sheet for 1,000 sets of sewing machines. We are enclosing our S/C No. 345 in duplicate. Please countersign one and return to us for our file.

(15) We are sending you our S/C Number 200 in duplicate, one copy of which please sign and return for our file.

(16) Enclosed is our sales confirmation Number 35 in duplicate. Please sign a copy and return for our file.

(17) We appreciate your order Number 308 for 3,000 pieces of women's shirts. We are pleased to accept your terms. Enclosed please find a copy of our Sales Confirmation Number 56-2019.

(18) During the past years we have made occasional purchases from your company, but we should now like to place regular orders.

(19) We are pleased to place a trial order and enclose our official order form.

(20) Thank you for your order NO. 32, and we are now dealing with it and you may expect delivery with a month.

II. Intermediate Training

1. Supply the missing words in the blanks of the following letter. The first letters are given.

Dear Sirs,

　　T____ you for your l____ of March 15th, in w____ you e____ specifications of your product BF847. We have seen the s____ and are p____ to place a t____ order if you can g____ shipment by May 10th.

The enclosed o____ is given strictly on the above c____, and we r____ the right of cancellation and refusal of d____ after this d____. Please let us k____ soon whether you can c____ acceptance of our order.

Yours faithfully,

× × ×

2. Cloze. Choose the most suitable words from the list of words to fill in the blanks. Each word can be used only once.

duplicate   order   terms   file   accept   enclosed   Contract   return

Dear Ms. Jennifer,

We appreciate your letter of September 20th, 2019 together with your ___(1)___ Number 38 for 300 tons of garlic.

We are pleased to ___(2)___ your ___(3)___ and conditions. ___(4)___ please find our Sales ___(5)___ Number 333 in ___(6)___. Please sign one copy and ___(7)___ to us for our ___(8)___.

We wish to point out that a letter of credit in our favour should be opened before October 20th, 2019.

Yours sincerely,

× × ×

3. Translate the following Chinese into English.

(1) 首次订购

(2) 达成交易

(3) 修改后的订单

(4) 执行订单

(5) 以……价格订购某物

(6) 销售合同

(7) 签退一份……供某人存档

(8) 一式两份

(9) 商业发票

(10) 收到……后

(11) 从你们7月5日寄来的样品中，我们已经作出了选择。很高兴向你方下订单。如质量合适，我们将来会向你方下续订单。

(12) 最近对我们的山地自行车需求甚多，我们不能保证新订货在6月30日之前交付。

(13) 请加速开立信用证，以便于我方能顺利执行订单。

(14) 关于你方2019年9月5日的来函，我们很高兴告知你方我们已经接受你们关于2,000台闹钟的订单。

(15) 我们很高兴附上销售合同第2068号一式二份，请你方签字并退回一份供我方备案。

(16) 附寄我方第589号合同正本两份。请将已会签的合同一份寄给我方。

(17) 因为存货售罄，我们不能接受新订单。但是一旦有新货源到来，我们即与你方联系。

(18) 我们正在执行你方678号订单。请相信我们定将在规定的期限内安排好装运。

(19) 如果你方能给我方5%的佣金，我方将试订500台。

(20) 你方6月15日订购2,000千克中国安哥拉兔毛的第89号订单收悉。非常感谢，我们欢迎你们成为我们的新客户。

Ⅲ. Advanced Training

 1. Translate the following letter into English.

敬启者：

感谢你方第181号订单，订购300台SP200型电视机。

我们很愿意为你方提供此货，但目前不能执行该订单，因为部分部件缺货。然而我方可提供品质非常类似的SP201型货品，可供现货。该型号仅次于SP200型，但价格低8%，可能更适合你方市场。

我们希望你方能采纳该建议。如能确认，我们会非常认真履行你方订单。

 2. Write an order covering the following contents.

(1) 有意订购对方公司的某牌号录像机、录像带、微型收录两用机

(2) 数量：录像机1,000台

　　　录像带1,000盒

　　　微型收录两用机5,000台

(3) 价格：FOB新港，包括我方5%佣金

　　　录像机：每台×美元

　　　录像带：每盒×美元

微型收录机:每台×美元

(4) 付款方式:90天期信用证装船前30天开立

(5) 包装:用标准出口箱包装

(6) 交货日期:一批或分二批8月底前交完

Module 4
Communication in Stage of Preparation of the Goods
备货阶段沟通

Unit 6　Establishment and Amendment of L/C
信用证的开立与修改

Lead-in

Try to finish the following tasks and find out the learning objectives of this unit.

Task 1

假设你是广州轻工业产品进出口公司的外贸业务员,最近你公司与英国一公司达成一笔交易,并收到了对方开立的信用证,但细读后发现装运条款与合同不符,因此,请代表公司致函对方公司,要求修改信用证。注意信中包含以下内容:

(1) 我方已收到你方由伦敦渣打银行开立的金额为 18,000 美元关于 15,000 打弹力尼龙袜的编号为 3639 的信用证。细读后,发现不允许分批装运和转运。

(2) 由于到达你方港口的直达轮稀少,我方不得不通过香港转运。同时,允许分批装运将对双方有利,因为我方可以随时将手头货物装运而不用等待整批货生产完成。因此,我方要求你方将信用证修改为"允许分批装运和转运"。

(3) 若你方能将信用证修改书尽快送达,我方将不胜感激,因为我们的货物已经备妥待运多时。

Task 2

假设你是杭州纺织品进出口公司的外贸业务员,最近你公司和美国一家贸易公司达成了一笔贸易,但交易达成后,对方迟迟未能开出相关信用证,以至于你们在收到相关信用证时已经因为太迟而无法按照合同规定的时间交货。现在,为保证合同的顺利履行,请代表公司致函该公司,要求对方延证。注意信中需包含以下内容:

(1) 我们遗憾地告诉你们,直到今天(2019 年 5 月 6 日)我方才收到贵公司有关标题销售确认书的信用证。

（2）确认书上清楚地规定有关信用证应于4月30日之前抵达我方。由于你方信用证的延迟，致使我方无法按合同规定的时间发货。

（3）鉴于我们长期友好的关系，我方仍愿装运你方所订货物，但需贵公司将信用证的装运期和有效期分别延长至6月15日和7月底。

（4）请贵公司务必在5月15日之前把信用证修改书寄达我方。否则，我方无法如期装运货物。

（5）盼及早收到贵方信用证修改通知书。

Part Ⅰ　Introduction

付款条件关系到双方的利益，应在合同中加以明确。付款方式主要有三种，即汇付（Remittance）、托收（Collection）及信用证（L/C）。

汇付属于顺汇性质，是进口人通过银行将货款汇交给出口人。根据不同的汇款方法，汇付方式有电汇（telegraphic transfer，T/T）、信汇（mail transfer，M/T）和票汇（remittance by banker's demand draft，D/D）。

托收属于逆汇性质，是出口人委托银行向进口人收款的一种方法。根据金融票据是否附带商业单据，分为光票托收（clean collection）和跟单托收（documentary collection）。跟单托收按交付货运单据条件的不同，又可分为付款交单（Documents against Payment，D/P）和承兑交单（Documents against Acceptance，D/A）。付款交单按支付时间不同又可分为即期付款交单（D/P at sight）和远期付款交单（D/P after sight）。

在三种付款方式中，使用最多的是凭信用证付款。由于凭信用证付款属于银行信用，银行承担第一付款的责任，对双方的利益都有保障，因此成为当今国际贸易常用的一种支付方式。

关于付款条件的函电主要涉及以下内容：

（1）开立信用证。进口商向银行申请开立信用证。

（2）催证。在临近开证日期而未收到信用证，出口商催促进口商按时开立信用证。

（3）改证。在出口商审证后，若发现信用证与合同不符，要求进口商修改信用证。

（4）展证。如果出口商不能及时交货，要求进口商延展信用证规定的交货期限或装运期限和有效期。

（5）催款。出口商在规定期限内未收到货款，提醒或催促进口人付款。

书写此类函电，要求语言简洁、语气诚恳，说明自己的意见，希望对方予以接受。

Part Ⅱ　Letter Writing Guide

1. For letters urging establishment of L/C 催证函

(1) Referring to the goods, relative order or contract

(2) Complaining about non-receipt of L/C; stating your urgent need for the L/C and inviting attention to the matter

(3) Urging the buyer to rush the opening of the L/C

(4) Expecting receiving L/C in early time

2. For letters advising establishment of L/C 通知信用证已开立

(1) Referring to the goods, relative order or contract

(2) Stating that you have instructed a bank to open an L/C, indicating the details of the L/C

(3) Expecting an early shipment

3. For letters asking for the amendment of L/C 改证函

(1) Telling the buyer that you have received the L/C

(2) Pointing out the discrepancies that need amendments

(3) Expecting an early amendment

4. For letters asking for the extension of L/C 展证函

(1) Telling the buyer that you have received the L/C

(2) Stating the reasons for extension

(3) Expecting an early amendment

5. For letters urging the advanced payment 催款函

(1) Referring to the goods, relative order or contract

(2) Complaining about non-receipt of advanced payment; stating your urgent need for advanced payment and inviting attention to the matter

(3) Urging the buyer to rush the paying of the advanced payment

(4) Expecting receiving advanced payment in early time

Part Ⅲ Sample Letters

1. Urging Establishment of L/C for Delivery Date is Approaching

Dear Sirs,

We wrote a letter to you on the 5th of August to confirm having received your order for 50 sets of Drilling Machines Type 684 and we, accordingly, enclosed the original of our Sales Confirmation No. DP511, which stipulates shipment be made by the end of October and the L/C reach us one month before the shipment date. Now the shipment date is approaching, but your L/C has not been received by us. We think your immediate attention should be called to this matter.

Therefore, we have to write to you again for urging your establishment of the above-mentioned L/C to enable us to execute your order smoothly.

We thank you for your cooperation.

Yours faithfully,

×××

Notes

1. drilling machine 钻孔机,钻机;钻床

    drill [dril] v. make (a hole, etc.) in some substance, esp. with a drill 钻孔

    e.g. They're drilling for oil off the Irish coast.

    他们在爱尔兰沿海钻井采油。

2. accordingly [ə'kɔːdiŋli] adv. therefore, for the reason (句首或句中)因此 in the manner that is suggested by what is known or has been said(句末)照办,相应地

    e.g. Our stocks are running low on account of heavy sales. Accordingly, we cannot offer you more than 10 tons.

    因为销量巨大,我们的库存正在减少。因此,我们无法提供10吨以上的货物。

    e.g. We have amended the credit accordingly.

    我们已相应地修改了信用证。

3. original [ə'ridʒənl] n. the original: the earliest form of sth. (from which copies can be made) 原作,原稿,原件;原型;原物

    e.g. This is a translation, because the original is in French.

    这是译文,因为原文是法语的。

4. stipulate ['stipjuleit] vt. state sth. clearly and firmly as a requirement 讲明;规定(某要求)

    e.g. It was stipulated that the goods should be delivered within three days.

    按规定货物需在三天内送交。

5. approach [ə'prəutʃ] vi./vt. come near or nearer to (sb./sth.) in space or time (在空间或时间上)接近,靠近(某人/某事物)

    e.g. As you approach the town, the first building you see is the church.

接近那座城镇的时候，首先看到的就是教堂。

6. urge [əːdʒ] vt. try earnestly or persistently to persuade sb. 诚恳或持续地催促，敦促；要求，通常用法为 sb. urge sth., sb. urge that..., sb. urge sb. to do sth.

   e.g. They urge the importance of punctual shipment.

   他们敦促准时装运的重要性。

   e.g. They urge that prompt attention be paid to the improvement of packing.

   他们要求立即处理包装的改进问题。

   e.g. As the duration of their license is short, the buyer urges you to hurry the shipment.

   由于许可证期限较短，买方催促你方尽快装运。

   e.g. The buyers urges the sellers to make an explanation.

   买方敦促卖方作出解释。

7. establishment [iˈstæbliʃmənt] n. 开立；建立

   establishment of an L/C 开立信用证

   establishment of a firm 建立公司

   establish [iˈstæbliʃ] vt. set(sth.) up on a firm or permanent basis 开立；建立；确立

   e.g. Please establish the covering L/C as soon as possible.

   请尽快开立相关信用证。

   e.g. We take the liberty of writing to you with a view to establish business relations with your firm.

   我们冒昧致函希望与贵公司建立业务关系。

   e.g. Our brand has been established in the European market.

   我们品牌在欧洲市场地位稳固。

8. the above-mentioned L/C 上述信用证　【同义】the above L/C, the said L/C, the captioned L/C

9. enable [iˈneibl] vt. 使(某人)能够，通常用法是 enable sb. to do sth.

   e.g. Please fax the amendment immediately so as to enable us to effect shipment in June.

   请立即将信用证修改书传真给我方，以使我方能够在六月装运。

10. execute [ˈeksikjuːt] vt. carry out, perform (what one is asked or told to do) 执行；实施；履行；完成

    execute the order 执行订单

    e.g. Please do your utmost to execute the order at an early date.

    请尽力及早执行订单。

    e.g. Please try your best to execute the order in exact accordance with the date of shipment as stipulated in the contract.

    请你方务必严格按照合同规定的装运日期执行订单。

2. Advising Establishment of L/C and Asking for Timely Delivery

Dear Sirs,

We are glad to inform you that we have now opened an irrevocable letter of credit through the Bank of Boston, Massachusetts, USA for US$ 150,000 in your favor.

Please make sure that the shipment is effected within September, since punctual delivery is one of the important consideration in dealing with our market.

We are awaiting your Shipping Advice.

Yours faithfully,

×××

 Notes

1. irrevocable [iˈrevəkəbl] *adj.* that can not be changed or revoked; final 不能改变的;不能取消的;不可撤销的;最后确定性的
   an irrevocable decision, judgment 不可改变的决定、判决
   an irrevocable letter of credit 不可撤销的信用证

2. Boston [ˈbɔstən] 波士顿,位于美国东北部大西洋沿岸,是美国东北部高等教育和医疗保健的中心,经济基础是科研、金融和技术,是一个全球性城市或世界性城市。世界学府哈佛大学和麻省理工学院都位于该市。

3. Massachusetts [mæsəˈtʃusits] 马萨诸塞州,是美国的一个州,首府是波士顿,位于美国东北部,是新英格兰地区的一部分,中文通常简称为麻省或麻州。

4. in favor of sb., in one's favor: payable to (the account of) sb. 以某人为受益人,以某人为受款人
   e.g. Cheques should be written in favor of Oxfam.
   支票上请写明以牛津饥荒救济委员会为受款人。
   e.g. We have opened an L/C in your favor through the Bank of China for the amount of US 18,000 dollars.
   我们已经通过中国银行开立了以你方为受益人的金额为 18,000 美元的信用证。

5. effect [iˈfekt] *vt.* bring (sth.) about; cause to occur 使(某事物)产生,使发生;引起
   effect a cure/ change/ sale 产生疗效/引起变化/实行大减价

effect shipment 安排装运

6. punctual ['pʌŋktʃuəl] *adj*. happening or doing sth. at the agreed or proper time 按时的；准时的；守时的

   be punctual for an appointment 准时赴约

   punctual delivery 准时交货

7. Shipping Advice 装运通知 【同义】Advice of Shipment，Shipment Notice，Notice of Shipment

   按照国际贸易的习惯做法，发货人在装运货物后，应立即发送装运通知给买方，将合同号、品名、件数、重量、金额、船名、装船的日期等告知买方，以便买方办理保险、做好报关接货的准备。

3. Amendment of L/C

（1）**Amendment of Shipment Terms**

Dear Mr. Bean，

We have received your L/C No. 3689 issued by the Chartered Bank，London for the amount of \$ 18,000 covering 18,000 dozen stretch nylon socks. On perusal，we find that transshipment and partial shipment are not allowed.

As direct steamers to your port are few and far between，we often have to ship via Hong Kong. It would be to mutual benefit to use partial shipment because we could ship immediately whatever we have on hand instead of waiting for the whole lot to be completed. Therefore，we are asking you to amend the L/C to read "Partial shipments and transshipment allowed".

We shall appreciate it if you will modify promptly the L/C as requested.

Yours sincerely，

×××

 Notes

1. issue ['iʃuː] *vt*. issue sth. (to sb.)/ issue sb. with sth.，supply or distribute sth. to sb. for use 将某物发给、供给或分配给某人使用

   issue visas to foreign visitors 给外国游客签证

2. Chartered Bank 渣打银行,是一家英国银行,建立于1853年,总部位于伦敦。

   charter ['tʃɑ:tə] n. written statement by a ruler or a government granting certain right and privilege to a town, company, university, etc. 特许状(统治者或政府给予一城市、公司、大学等的某些权利或特权的证书)

   chartered ['tʃɑ:təd] adj. qualified according to the rules of a professional association which has a royal charter(根据持有皇家特许状的专业协会的规章)合格的

   a chartered engineer/ surveyor 特许工程师/检测官

3. stretch nylon socks 弹力尼龙袜

   stretch [stretʃ] n. ability to be stretched; elasticity 伸展的能力;弹性;伸缩性

   stretch jeans, seat-covers, underwear 弹力牛仔裤、椅套、内衣

   nylon ['nailɔn] n. very strong man-made fibre used for hosiery, rope, brushes, etc. 尼龙

   nylon tights, blouses, etc. 尼龙裤袜、女衬衫等

4. on perusal 在细读/详阅之后

   perusal [pə'ru:zl] n. (action of) reading carefully 细读

5. transshipment [træns'ʃipmənt] n. 转船装运

   trans-(pref.)前缀 (1)(与形容词连用) across; beyond 横穿;通过;超越 transatlantic 横跨大西洋的 (2)(与动词连用) into another place or state 进入另一处或另一种状态 transplant 移植;移栽,移种;移居 transform 改变形态;改变外观

6. partial shipments 分批装运

   partial ['pɑ:ʃl] adj. of or forming a part; not complete 部分的;不完全的

   a partial recovery/ success 部分复原/成功

   e.g. We enclose a check in partial payment for the goods shipped on consignment. 随函附寄一张支票,作为所装运来的寄售货物的部分款项。

7. steamer ['sti:mə] n. a steamer is a ship that has an engine powered by steam 汽船;轮船

8. few and far between: not frequent; not happening often 稀少,稀疏;不常发生

   e.g. In the 19th century, railroads were few and far between. 在十九世纪,铁路还很罕见。

9. via ['vaiə] prep. (拉丁语)经由 【同义】by way of, through

   e.g. The goods will shipped via Hong Kong. 货物将经由香港转运。

   e.g. The samples were sent via airmail. 样品已通过航空邮件寄出。

10. mutual ['mju:tʃuəl] adj. (of feeling or an action) felt or done by each towards the other (指感想或行为)相互的;彼此的

    mutual aid/ assistance/ suspicion 相互援助/帮助/猜疑

11. lot [lɔt] n. a group or set of people or things 组,群,批,套

lot number 批号

e.g. The first lot of visitors has arrived.

首批游客已经到达。

12. read [ri:d] v. [动词 + 直接引语] to have sth. written on it; to be written in a particular way 写着;写成;写有某字样

e.g. The sign reads "No admittance".

告示牌上写着"禁止入内"。

e.g. I've changed the last paragraph. It now reads as follows ...

我已经修改了最后一段。现在是这样写的……

13. modify ['mɔdifai] vt. change sth. slightly, esp to make it less extreme or to improve it 稍改(某事物);更改,修改;(使)改善,(使)改进

modify the terms of a contract 修改合同条款

e.g. The software we use has been modified for us.

我们使用的软件已按我们的需求做过修改。

 (2) Asking the Buyer to Cancel the Request of Manufacturer's Certificate

Dear Sirs,

Re: Your Letter of Credit No. 5656

We have received your captioned Letter of Credit.

Among the clauses specified in your credit we find that the following two points do not conform to the relative contract:

① Your L/C calls for Manufacturer's Certificate, which is not included in the contract. In fact, the contracted commodity is a kind of agricultural produce. It is impossible to obtain manufacturer's certificate.

② The contract number should be 19/1245 instead of 18/1245.

As the goods are now ready for shipment, you are requested to amend your credit as soon as possible.

Yours faithfully,

×××

 Notes

1. captioned ['kæpʃənd] adj. 标题下的

2. specify ['spesifai] vt. state or name clearly and definitely (details, materials, etc.) 确切说明(细节、材料等);明确规定;详述

e.g. Remember to specify your size when ordering clothes.
订购服装时记着要详细说明你要的尺码。

3. conform [kən'fɔ:m] vi. 遵守;遵从

(1) conform to sth.: keep to or comply with (generally accepted rules, standards, etc.) 符合或遵守(公认的规则、准则等)

e.g. The building does not conform to safety regulations.
这座建筑不符合安全条例。

(2) conform to/ with sth.: agree or be consistent with sth. 与某事物相符合、相一致

e.g. His ideas do not conform with mine.
他的想法和我的不一致。

4. Manufacturer's Certificate 生产厂家证明

5. produce ['prɔdju:s] n. things that have been produced, esp. by farming 产品,尤指农产品

farm produce 农产品

e.g. The shop sells only fresh local produce.
这家商店专售当地的新鲜农产品。

 (3) **Asking to Amend the Amount and Packing Terms**

Dear Sirs,

Re: L/C No. 345 Issued by First National City Bank

We have received the above L/C in payment for your Order No. 678 covering 200 cases of …

When we checked the L/C with the relevant contract, we found that the amount on your L/C is insufficient. The correct total CIF New York value of your order comes to US$ 2,750.00 instead of US$ 2,550.00, the difference being US$ 200.00.

Your L/C allows us only half a month to effect delivery, but as we have agreed in the contract, the delivery should be made within one month after receipt of the L/C.

As to packing, the contract stipulates that the goods should be packed in cartons and reinforced with nylon straps outside, but your L/C required metal straps instead. We think we should arrange the packing according to the contract.

In view of the above, you are kindly requested to increase the amount of your L/C by US$ 200.00, extend the shipment and validity to September 15th and 30th respectively, as well as amend the terms of packing. Meanwhile please advise us as soon as possible.

Yours faithfully,

×××

Notes

1. First National City Bank 第一国家城市银行,现更名为 Citibank,即花旗银行,总部位于纽约,是美国最大的银行之一。

2. cover ['kʌvə] vt. include (sth.); deal with 包括(某事物);涉及;处理;适用于
   the sales team covering the northern part of the country
   负责这个国家北部地区的销售队伍
   e.g. The survey covers all aspects of the business.
   调查包括这家企业的各种方面。

3. relevant ['reləvənt] adj. relevant to sth./sb. connected with what is being discussed, what is happening, what is being done, etc. 有关的;切题的
   have all the relevant documents ready 已把一切有关文件准备妥当
   supply the facts relevant to the case 提供与该案有关的事实

4. insufficient [in'səfiʃənt] adj. insufficient for sth., insufficient to do sth. 不充足的,不充分的,不够的
   e.g. His salary is insufficient to meet his needs.
   他的薪水不够应付需要。
   e.g. The case was dismissed because of insufficient evidence.
   该案因证据不足而撤销。

5. receipt [ri'si:t] n. acting of receiving or being received 收到
   to acknowledge receipt of a letter 确认信已收到
   e.g. The goods will be dispatched on receipt of an order form.
   订单一到即发货

6. reinforce [ri:in'fɔ:s] vt. make sth. stronger by adding material, etc. (以添加材料等)加固(某物)
   e.g. All buildings are now reinforced to withstand earthquakes.
   所有建筑现都已加固,以抗地震。

7. strap [stræp] n. a strip of leather, cloth or other material that is used to fasten sth. 带子(用皮、布等做成)

a watch with a leather strap 皮表带的手表

8. validity [vəˈlidəti] n. state of being legally acceptable （法律上）有效；合法性

   e.g. The period of validity of the agreement has expired.
   本协议的有效期已过。

9. respectively [risˈpektivli] adv. separately or in turn, in the order mentioned 各自地；分别地；轮流地

   e.g. They finished first and second respectively.
   他们分获一二名。

10. terms [tə:mz] n. (pl.) conditions offered or accepted（提出的或接受的）条件

    according to the terms of the contract 按照合同的条件

    e.g. Under the terms of agreement, their funding of the project will continue until 2020.
    根据协议条款，他们为这个项目提供资金，直到2020年为止。

11. advise [ədˈvaiz] vt. inform or notify sb. 通知或告知某人，通常用于 advise sb. (of sth.)

    e.g. Please advise us of the dispatch of the goods.
    货物发出请通知我们。

    e.g. Please advise us of any change of address.
    如地址有变，敬请告知。

4. Extension of L/C

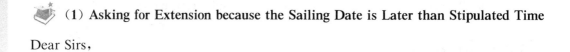 (1) Asking for Extension because the Sailing Date is Later than Stipulated Time

Dear Sirs,

We have received your L/C No. AG4521 for the amount of $ 2,960 to cover your Order No. 860 for 20 metric tons of ...

The said credit calls for shipment on or before December 31st. As the earliest steamer sailing for your port is S. S. "PEACE" scheduled to leave Shanghai on or about January 3rd next year, it is, therefore, impossible for us to effect shipment at the time you named.

This being the case, we have to ask you to extend the date of shipment to January 15th, and advise us in time.

Yours faithfully,

×××

Notes

1. metric ton n. 公吨（1 公吨等于 1,000 千克）
2. this being the case 事实既然如此，也可以表达为 such being the case。
3. extend [ik'stend] vt. make (sth.) longer or larger (in space or time) 使（某物）（在空间或时间上）更大，更长，伸长，延长，延展

   extend the deadline until the end of the month 延期到月底截止

   extension [ik'stenʃən] n. 更大，更长，伸长，延长，延展

   the extension of a contract 合同有效期的延长

   the extension of a loan 贷款偿还期的延长

 （2）Asking for Extension because Goods are not Ready

Dear Sirs，

We thank you for your L/C No. 244 for five metric tons of frozen rabbit meat. We are sorry that owing to the delay on the part of our suppliers, we are unable to get the goods ready before the end of this month, so we write to you asking for an extension of the L/C.

It is expected that the consignment will be ready for shipment in the early part of May and we are arranging to ship it on S. S. "Red Star" sailing from Shanghai on May 10th.

We are looking forward to receiving your extension of the above L/C, thus enabling us to effect shipment of the goods in question.

Yours faithfully,

×××

Notes

1. consignment [kən'sainmənt] n. consigning; goods consigned 发运、托运；所运送之物

   a new consignment of goods 新到的一批货

   consignment business 寄售业务；委托买卖

2. the early part of May 五月上旬

   英语无上、中、下旬的说法，因此上旬可意译如上。下旬可译为 the late part of a month 或 late in a month，五月中旬可译为 mid-May。

3. ship [ʃip] vt. send or transport (sth./sb.), esp. in a ship 运送（某人、某物）（尤指用船）

e.g. The company ships its goods all over the world.

公司把货物运往世界各地。

e.g. We ship grain to Africa.

我们把谷物运往非洲。

4. in question 所涉及的

e.g. The goods in question have been in good demand since the beginning of the year.

自本年初以来该货一直畅销。

5. Urging Deposit and Balance

 (1) Urging Deposit

Dear Jan,

Last time we confirmed the PI, here I want to know when you can arrange the deposit? Once we received the deposit we will arrange the production. We do have many orders recently. Since you order so many items and different colors, we should try to arrange the production with other orders, so that we can guarantee the time of delivery.

We look forward to your early reply.

Best regards,

Kelly Yang

 Notes

1. PI (Proforma Invoice) 形式发票

   PO (Purchase Order) 订货单

   很多客户在谈判完成后下单,会有正式的合同,也就是我们常说的PO。这时供应商会核对相关内容,提出接受或修改意见,然后和客户协商。这时,PO就是真正意义上的合同。但即便如此,供应商还是尽量再做一份PI给客户确认,因为PO是客户做的,客户的意思有时会跟供应商的理解有偏差,若仅回签PO,以后若对于合同的条款发生争议,就会产生麻烦。

   PI虽然只是形式发票,但很多客户都把PI当成正式合同,双方签署的任何PI都是有效的。有些客户没有PO给供应商,只要求供应商根据确定好的产品、价格、交货期等做好PI给他确认,一旦确认,就等同于真正的合同。当然,还有少部分客户,只把PI理解成一个正式的报价单,并非合同或形式发票。

2. deposit [di'pɔzit] n. payment of a part of a larger sum, the rest of which is to be paid

later 定金；定钱

e.g. The shop promised to keep the goods for me if I paid a deposit.

商店答应，如果我付定金就给我保留这批货。

e.g. We have put down a 5% deposit on the house.

我们已支付了房款的5%作为定金。

3. guarantee [ˌɡærənˈtiː] v. guarantee sth. (to sb.) promise sth. with certainty (to sb.) (向某人)保证

e.g. We cannot guarantee the punctual arrival of trains in foggy weather.

我们不能保证火车在雾天正点达到。

e.g. We guarantee you delivery within one day.

我们担保你在一日内收到。

 (2) Urging Balance

Dear Jan，

Attached here is your mass production decking pictures. Our production is almost ready and the goods are ready to be delivered.

Here please arrange the balance payment.

You have remitted us USD 6,694 as deposit，the balance is USD 17,419，including 1,800 USD freight cost from our port to Stavanger Port.

Once we received your balance，we will arrange the booking of shipping space.

We look forward to hearing from you soon.

Best regards，

Kelly Yang

 Notes

1. mass production: production of sth. in large quantities，esp. by machine(尤指机器进行的)批量生产，大量生产

2. decking [ˈdekɪŋ] n. wooden boards that are fixed to the ground in a garden or other outdoor area for people to walk on (屋外花园等处)木质铺面(板)

3. balance [ˈbæləns] n. amount of money still owed after some payment has been made 余

欠之钱数,余款

e.g. The balance of $ 500 will be paid within one week. 500 美元的余款将在一周之内付清。

4. remit [ri'mit] vt. remit sth. (to sb.) send (money, etc.) to a person or place, esp. by post 汇(款等)

e.g. Kindly remit the balance without delay.
请立即将余额汇来。

e.g. Payment will be remitted to you in full.
款项将全额汇寄给你。

5. freight [freit] n. the movement of goods by lorries, trains, ships, or aeroplanes 货运

e.g. France derives 16% of revenue from air freight.
法国16%的税收来自航空货运。

6. Stavanger [stə'væŋə] n. 斯塔万格,挪威第四大城市,挪威西海岸的港口城市

7. shipping space n. 船位,舱位

Part Ⅳ Useful Expressions and Sentences

Expressions

1. D/P：documents against payment 付款交单

2. D/A：documents against acceptance 承兑交单

3. T/T：telegraphic transfer 电汇

4. C/D：cash against documents 凭单付现

5. establishment of an L/C 信用证的开立

6. execute the order 执行订单

7. irrevocable L/C 不可撤销信用证

8. in one's favour 以某人为受益人

9. effect shipment 安排装运

10. punctual delivery 准时交货

11. Shipping Advice 装运通知

12. on perusal 细读之后

13. transshipment and partial shipment 转运和分批装运

14. few and far between 稀少,稀疏

15. conform to sth. 符合或遵守（公认的规则、准则等）；与某事物相符合、相一致

16. this being the case 事实既然如此

17. PI：Proforma Invoice 形式发票
18. PO：Purchase Order 订货单
19. urge deposit 催付定金
20. urge balance 催付余款

Typical Sentences

1. As the goods against your order No. 005 have been ready for quite some time, it is imperative that you take immediate action to have the covering L/C established as soon as possible.

2. Please do your utmost to expedite L/C, so that shipment would be effected in July.

3. Please insert the word "about" before the quantity in your L/C No. 789.

4. Please amend the credit as allowing transshipment.

5. We have received your L/C No. 524, but we find it contains the following discrepancies: ... We would therefore request you to instruct your bank to make the necessary amendment.

6. As there is no direct sailing from Shanghai to your port during April/ May, it is imperative for you to delete the clause "by direct steamer" and insert the word "Partial shipments and transshipment are allowed".

7. The commission granted for this transaction is 3% as stipulated in our Sales Confirmation, but we find that your L/C demands a commission of 5%. Therefore, you are requested to instruct your bank to amend the L/C.

8. Owing to the late arrival of the steamer on which we have booked space, we would appreciate your extending the shipment date and validity of your L/C No. 4985 to January 31st and February 15th respectively.

9. We have received your L/C No. 1451 for USD 5,000 but find that Art. No. 1001 mentioned therein does not agree with what is contracted. The correct Art. No. should be 1002. Please make the amendment accordingly.

10. Please amend your L/C No. 886 to include the wording "5% more or less" under the items of quantity and amount.

Part Ⅴ Practical Training

Ⅰ. Elementary Training

1. Choose the best answer.

(1) When the goods are ready, the shipping agent will ____ and ____ them to the docks.
   A. deliver, collect   B. collect, send
   C. deliver, send   D. collect, deliver

(2) We wish to discuss with you some other important things if you could come ____ your earliest convenience.
   A. by   B. on   C. in   D. at

(3) Unfortunately, quite a number of the users are dissatisfied ____ your Straw Baskets under order No. 789.
   A. to   B. with   C. on   D. above

(4) They had decided to allow a 15% discount to avoid ____ another old customer of theirs.
   A. loss   B. lose   C. losing   D. lost

(5) We would like to express our satisfaction ____ receiving the first order and ____ prompt shipment of the goods.
   A. with, confirming   B. to, confirm
   C. at, confirm   D. in, confirming

(6) Will you please remit the extra charges to the Citibank New York ____ our credit?
   A. by   B. for   C. across   D. over

(7) Your products ____ so well here but for a lot of advertisements we have done on television and in newspapers.
   A. would not have been sold B. won't sell
   C. would not sell   D. have not been sold

(8) We have received orders ____ USD 2,000,000.00 since the new product was introduced to the market.
   A. amount for   B. amount to   C. account for   D. amounting to

(9) An L/C should be opened ____ our favor available by documentary draft ____

sixty days' sight.

A. in, for   B. in, after   C. on, in   D. in, at

(10) The stipulation of the L/C should ___ those of the contract.

A. agree to   B. agree in   C. agree on   D. agree with

(11) The correct total CFR value of your order comes to USD 3,928.00 instead of 9,328.00, the difference ___ USD 5,400.00.

A. be   B. is to be   C. being   D. been

(12) Please extend this letter of credit, which expires ___ January 25th.

A. on   B. in   C. at   D. for

(13) Thank you for your remittance of USD 2,150.00 ___ the 80% freight due under Invoice No. 228.

A. of paying   B. pay for   C. for payment for   D. in payment of

2. Read the following letters and fill in each blank with prepositions.

Letter 1

Dear Sirs,

Your L/C No. 1368 issued by the Bank of Tokyo has been received with many thanks.

After checking the L/C, we regret __(1)__ find some discrepancies which do not conform __(2)__ the contract, and would, therefore, request you to make the following amendments:

(1) The applicant should read "Tokyo Food Imp. & Exp. Co., Ltd." not "Tokyo Imp. & Exp. Co., Ltd."

(2) The amount both in figure and in word should respectively be Stg £100,000(say Pounds Sterling One Hundred Thousand only) instead of US$ 100,000(say US Dollars One Hundred Thousand only)

(3) "FOBC 2% Dalian" instead __(3)__ "FOB Dalian"

(4) Please delete insurance clause.

(5) Please insert "on or about" before "April 10th".

(6) The L/C should be negotiated in China rather than in Japan.

As the goods have been ready for a long time, please expedite the amendment so that we can ship the goods __(4)__ time.

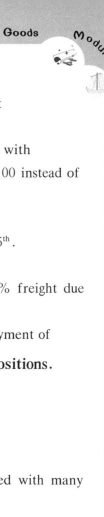

Thank you ___(5)___ advance for your cooperation.

Yours sincerely,

× × ×

Letter 2

Dear Sirs,

L/C No. 1399

Thank you ___(1)___ sending us the subject L/C.

We feel regretful that, as the factory has been understaffed since the Spring Festival, we are unable ___(2)___ ship the goods before June 15th, 2019 as contracted. ___(3)___ such circumstances, we would like you to extend the date of shipment and validity ___(4)___ the L/C ___(5)___ July 5th, 2019 and July 20th, 2019 respectively.

It will be highly appreciated if you will understand our position and give us your assistance.

Sincerely yours,

× × ×

 3. Translate the following English into Chinese.

(1) urge the establishment of L/C

(2) cash against shipping documents

(3) documentary L/C

(4) documents against payment

(5) documents against acceptance

(6) remittance

(7) on perusal

(8) extension of L/C

(9) draw a draft on sb.

(10) in one's favour

(11) We always adopt this kind of payment terms in our foreign trade.

(12) This point has been stipulated in the contract.

(13) It is necessary to check up the L/C with the contract.

(14) Payment by an irrevocable L/C was agreed upon by both parties.

(15) On request the shipment validity has been extended till the end of September.

(16) Thank you for your Letter of Credit No. 421. On perusal, we find it contains the following discrepancies.

(17) The goods should be insured for 110% of the invoice value, not 150%.

(18) It appears that the quantity in your L/C No. 355 does not agree with the contracted terms. Please rush amendments.

(19) Please amend the above L/C to read "shipment from Dalian" instead of "shipment from Qingdao".

(20) It would be greatly appreciated if you could extend the shipment and validity of L/C No. 124 to September 15th and October 31st respectively.

II. Intermediate Training

1. Supply the missing words in the blanks of the following letter. The first letters are given.

Dear Madam or Sir,

We wish to i____ you that the goods u____ L/C Number 46 have been r____ for quite some time. According to the s____ in the foregoing sales confirmations, s____ is to be made during May/June. However, we have not yet r____ your L/C even though you promised to e____ it immediately after signing the S____. We must p____ out that unless your L/C reaches us by the end of this month, we will not be able to e____ shipment within the stipulated time.

Please look into this matter and let us have a reply without delay.

Yours sincerely,

× × ×

2. Cloze. Choose the most suitable words from the list of words to fill in the blanks. Each word can be used only once.

payments   issued   upon   credit   trade
pay   importer   order   bills   negotiate

A major part of international __(1)__ is made either by __(2)__ of exchange or by documentary credit or a combination of the two. A documentary credit is a letter __(3)__ by a bank at the request of an importer of goods in which the bank promises to pay a beneficiary __(4)__ presentation of documents relating to the dispatch of goods. A letter of credit is sometimes just called credit, L/C for short. The commercial letter of credit is almost always a documentary __(5)__ in that it specifies the documents required such as bill of lading, an invoice and an insurance document plus one or two supplementary documents. If these documents are in __(6)__ and shipment has been made as specified on the credit, the bank will __(7)__ for the consignment in exchange for the documents or will accept a bill of exchange and, possibly, __(8)__ it. In international __(9)__, the importer and the exporter must arrange payment after having worked out an agreement. The __(10)__ will want possession of the merchandise before paying, and the exporter will want payment before making delivery. Since each party is far away from the other and often has an incomplete knowledge of its counterpart, there must be a certain caution to their dealings.

3. Translate the following Chinese into English.

(1) 开证申请人

(2) 开证行

(3) 通知行

(4) 受益人

(5) 议付行

(6) 不符点

(7) 信用证修改书

(8) 托收

(9) 保兑的、不可撤销的信用证

(10) 承兑交单

(11) 请尽力加快开证，以便我们能顺利地执行订单。

(12) 为了避免往后的修改，请务必做到信用证的规定与合同的条款完全一致。

(13) 如贵方能毫不延误地电开信用证修改书，我们将不胜感激，因为我方的货物已备妥待运多时。

(14) 请务必下月初开立信用证,并允许转船和分批装运。

(15) 请在信用证上加上下列条款"允许2%溢短装"。

(16) 请将信用证中的装船期和有效期分别延展至7月15日和8月15日,以便我们能顺利地执行该货物的装运。

(17) 我方发现你方9985号信用证金额短缺500英镑,请按合同金额予以修改。

(18) 关于信用证3215号,请删除"银行费用由受益人承担"的条款。

(19) 请你方支付发票金额的30%作为预付款,一收到你方预付款,我方将安排备货生产。

(20) 货物已备妥,请你方尽快付清余款。付完款后,请通知我方。

Ⅲ. Advanced Training

 1. Translate the following letter into English.

敬启者:

关于20公吨蛤蜊的158号信用证已收到,谢谢!经我方审核,你方信用证有下列两点与合同不符:

(1) 信用证中的价格应该为每公吨1,500美元,而不是每公吨1,300美元。

(2) 合同号为EX0304而不是EX0403。

请立即修改信用证。

谨上

 2. Check the following letters of credit with the contract terms given and then write a letter in English asking for amendment.

Irrevocable L/C from New York Bank

No. SDS 120

Date and place of issue: July 20th, 2018, New York

Date and place of expiry: October 20th, 2018, New York

Applicant: New York Imp. & Exp. Co., Ltd.

Beneficiary: South Export Corp., Shanghai

Advising Bank: Bank of China, Shanghai Branch

Amount: USD 10,000 (SAY US DOLLARS TEN THOUSAND ONLY)

Partial shipments and transshipment are prohibited.

Shipment from China Port to New York, latest September 30th, 2018.

Credit available against presentation of the following documents and of your draft at sight for 90% of the invoice value;

Signed commercial invoice in triplicate.

Full set of clean on board ocean Bills of Lading made of to order of New York Bank marked freight prepaid.

Insurance certificate or policy endorsed in blank for full invoice value plus 10%, covering All Risks and War Risk.

Covering 5 M/Ts Fresh Shrimps, first grade, at USD 2,000 per M/T CIF New York as per Contract No. 345C.

345C 号合同主要条款：

卖方：上海南方出口公司

买方：纽约食品进出口有限公司

5 公吨一级冻虾，每公吨 CIF 2,200 美元，2018 年 9 月 30 日前由中国港口用直达轮运往纽约。保险由卖方按发票金额 110% 投保一切险和战争险。凭不可撤销的即期信用证支付。

Module 5
Communication before and after Shipment
货物出运前后沟通

Unit 7 Shipment
装　运

Lead-in

Try to finish the following tasks and find out the learning objectives of this unit.

Task 1

　　假设你是美国巴特勒进出口公司的经理 Butler 先生。最近你公司和中国上海的宝来实业有限公司达成了订购 5,000 台电风扇的交易。由于你方客户的迫切需要,你希望上海公司可以提前发货。现在,请代表你们公司向上海的合作伙伴发函说明情况,并提出要求,注意信中务必包含以下内容:
　　(1) 关于 5,000 台电风扇订单的装运事宜,我方非常迫切地想知道具体的发运情况。
　　(2) 由于我方顾客的迫切需要,能否恳请贵方将装运期从 3 月 20 日提早到 3 月 10 日。
　　(3) 提出这样的要求实属无奈,希望能够见谅。
　　(4) 期待能尽早收到货物。

Task 2

　　假设你是上海宝来实业有限公司的销售经理,接到上述信件并权衡各方面因素之后,你认为你们公司没有办法确保提前发货。现在,为保证订单的顺利进行,请致函该公司,向其说明情况。注意信中务必包含以下内容:
　　(1) 来函收悉,谢谢!
　　(2) 很遗憾告诉贵方,我们无法按照你们的要求将装运时间提前。
　　(3) 每月只能停靠你方港口一次的直达班轮刚刚离开,船务公司告诉我们在 3 月 20 日前都没有空舱可提供。货物只能在 3 月 20 日才能装运。
　　(4) 我们很想满足贵方的要求,但这实在是超出了我们的能力范围,希望能够理解。
　　(5) 一旦货物装运,我们会及时电告船名及预计抵达时间。

Part I Introduction

1. 国际贸易的主要运输方式

在国际贸易中,货物可以通过多种方式进行运输,如海洋运输、航空运输、铁路运输、公路运输和管道运输等。其中,海洋运输是国际贸易中最主要的运输方式。

海洋运输具有运量大、不受道路限制的优点,可以降低单位商品运费,因此成为国际贸易中最主要的运输方式。其中集装箱班轮运输是海洋运输方式中最常用的一种。班轮运输中,船公司按固定航线、固定停靠港口、固定的航行时间表航行,按相对固定的运费率收取运费。

航空运输的优点是交货迅速,缺点是运量小、运输费用较高。航空运输适合于鲜活商品、急需商品,以及价值高而体积、重量较小的商品。班机运输是航空运输中主要的运输方式。航空运输的承运人是航空运输公司或航空货运代理公司。

铁路运输的特点是运量大、安全可靠,但仅限于有陆路相连接的国家。我国的国际铁路运输路线主要有两条:一是西伯利亚大陆桥。二是新亚欧大陆桥。新亚欧大陆桥由江苏连云港经过新疆与哈萨克斯坦铁路连接,贯穿俄罗斯、波兰、德国至荷兰的鹿特丹(又称新丝绸之路)。

2. 货物的装运

在卖方将货物准备好后,就要在合同或信用证规定的时间内将货物装运。装运涉及的工作环节有:托运、订舱、投保、报关、装运货物和发装运通知等。

采用不同的贸易术语时,买方和卖方承担不同的运输责任。在采用FOB术语或其他F组术语时,由买方安排运输工具;而采用CIF、CFR术语或其他C组术语时,由卖方安排运输工具并将货物装运。装运过程中,买卖双方要及时进行沟通,保证货物按时装运并及时到达目的地。

通常,一封装运函电会涉及两个主体,即买方和卖方。因此,由函电主体区分,装运函电可分为买方-卖方(Buyer to Seller)和卖方-买方(Seller to Buyer)两种。

Part II Letter Writing Guide

1. For letters of requiring shipping instructions 提出装运指示

(1) Referring to the shipment of the ordered goods.

(2) Providing the specific and detailed shipping requirements.

(3) Showing expects of receiving the goods in early time.

2. For letters of packing requirements 包装要求

(1) Referring to the shipment of the ordered goods.

(2) Providing the specific and detailed packing requirements.

(3) Showing expects of receiving the goods in early time.

3. For letters of urging shipment 催促尽早发货

(1) Stating the purpose of the letter directly: inquire about the shipment of the ordered goods.

(2) Urging shipment and giving reasons.

(3) Expressing the hope of receiving the goods as soon as possible.

4. For letters of applying 3rd Party for Inspection 申请第三方验货

(1) Referring to the shipment of the ordered goods.

(2) Expressing the willingness of applying 3rd party for inspection.

(3) Showing expectations of receiving the goods in early time.

5. For letters of shipping advice 装运通知

(1) Informing of shipment and name of vessel.

(2) Enclosing copies of the shipping documents.

(3) Expressing the hope that the goods will arrive in time and the business will continue to grow.

Part Ⅲ   Sample Letters

1. Shipping Instructions

 (1) Require to Book a Steamer from an Appointed Transportation Company

Dear Sirs,

<u>Re: Our Order No.123</u>

We have received your fax of March 2nd and noted that you have booked our Order No. 123 for 4 sets of Model 780 Machine. Our confirmation of the order will be

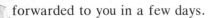 forwarded to you in a few days.

It is of great importance to our buyers that the arrival date of this order should be arranged as early as possible to meet their requirements, so you are supposed to ship the goods by a steamer of ✱ ✱ ✱ Co. The main reason is that their steamers offer the shortest time for the journey between China and England. We shall appreciate it if you will endeavor to ship the consignments as follows:

Order No. 123: by S. S. "✱ ✱ ✱" due to sail from London on April 18th, 2018 or latest by S. S. "✱ ✱ ✱" due to sail from London on May 18th, 2018 arriving in Amoy on May 30th, 2018 and June 15th, 2018 respectively.

Thank you in advance for your cooperation.

Yours faithfully,

×××

 Notes

1. endeavour [inˈdevə; en-] n. 努力;尽力　vi. attempt by employing effort 努力;尽力;力图

   do one's endeavour 尽力,竭力

   make every endeavour 尽一切努力

   make one's best endeavour 尽最大努力

   e. g. Please make every endeavour to arrive punctually.

   请尽量准时到达。

   e. g. They are endeavouring to protect trade union rights.

   他们正在努力保护工会权利。

2. due [djuː] adj.

   (1) scheduled to arrive, suitable to or expected in the circumstances（车、船等）预定应到的;预期的;约定的

   e. g. When are the goods due at Xingang?

   货物应该什么时候到达新港?

   e. g. The ship is due to leave on or about May 10th.

   该轮预计5月10号或左右离港。

   (2) owed and payable immediately or on demand（票据等）到期的

   e. g. The borrower should pay the principle as well as the interests when the loan becomes due.

当贷款到期时,借方应付本金和利息。

 (2) **Instructions for Shipping Marks**

Dear Sirs,

<u>Re: Our Order No. 165</u>

With reference to the shipment of our Order No. 165 for 100 cases of China Wares, we wish to draw your attention to the following:

As the goods are susceptible to be broken, the wares must be packed in wooden cases capable of withstanding rough handling.

Please mark the cases with our initials in a diamond, under which comes the destination with contract number and stencil conspicuously the words "FRAGILE, HANDLE WITH CARE" on both sides of the cases.

We trust that the above instructions are clear to you and that the shipment will give the users entire satisfaction.

Yours faithfully,

 Notes

1. with reference to ... (常用于商业书信的开头,表示事由)兹谈及…… 【同义】We refer to ... referring to ...; make reference to reference is made to ...

   e.g. Referring to your fax of March 3rd ordering 500 M/T of Groundnut Kernels.
   兹谈及你方3月3日订购500公吨花生仁的来函。

2. susceptible [səˈseptib(ə)l] *adj*. easily impressed emotionally 易受影响的;可被……的;可受……影响的

   e.g. Young people are the most susceptible to advertisements.
   年轻人最容易受广告影响。

   e.g. James was extremely susceptible to flattery.
   詹姆斯非常容易受奉承话的影响。

3. withstand [wiðˈstænd] *vt*. resist or confront with resistance; stand up or offer resistance to somebody or something 抵挡;反抗;顶得住,经受住

shoes that will withstand hard wear 耐穿的鞋

e.g. If you believe it is fair for all concerned, it will withstand the test of time.
如果你相信它从任何观点考量都是公平的,它将会经得起时间的考验。

2. Packing Requirements

Dear Sirs,

We regret to inform you that the 150 cartons of Iron Nails you shipped Dubai on April 12th, 2019 were badly damaged, of course through no fault of yours.

We are now writing to you in regard to the packing of these nails, which we feel necessary to clarify for our future dealings.

The packing for Dubai is to be in cartons of 110 lbs net, each containing 6 lbs × 16 packets. For Malta, we would like you to have the goods packed in double gunny bags of 50/60 kilos each. As for the British market, our buyers prefer 25-kilo cartons.

Kindly let us know whether these requirements could be met.

Yours faithfully,

× × ×

 Notes

1. packing ['pækiŋ] n. any material used especially to protect something 包装
   packing charges 包装费用   packing instructions 包装要求,包装须知
   packing list 装箱单   exporter packing 出口包装
   inner packing 内包装   outer packing 外包装
   neutral packing 中性包装
   部分常用的出口包装容器名称:

bag 袋,包	gunny bag 麻袋	polybag 塑料袋
bale 包,布包	barrel 琵琶桶	box 盒,箱
bundle 捆	carton 纸板箱	case 箱
wooden case 木箱	cask 木桶	crate 板条箱
drum 铁皮圆桶	keg 小圆桶	tin(英)= can(美)听,罐头

pack v. arrange in a container 包装

(1) in ... 用某种容器包装

e.g. Walnuts are packed in double gunny bags.

核桃用双层麻袋包装

(2) in ... of ... each 用某种容器包装,每件若干

e.g. Men's shirts are packed in cartons of 10 dozen each.

男士衬衫用纸箱包装,每箱10打。

(3) in ..., each containing 用某种容器包装,每件内装若干

e.g. Nylon Socks are packed in cartons, each containing 80 dozens.

尼龙袜用纸箱包装,每箱装80打。

(4) ... to ... 若干件装于一件某容器

e.g. Folding chairs are packed 2 pieces to a carton.

折叠椅两把装一个纸板箱。

(5) each ... in ... and ... to ... 每单位装某种容器,若干单位装另一种较大的容器

e.g. Each pair of Nylon Socks is packed in a polybag and 12 pairs to a box.

每双尼龙袜装一个塑料袋,12双装一盒。

(6) ... to ... and ... to ... 若干单位装某种容器,若干此种容器装另一种较大的容器

e.g. Pens are packed 10 pieces to a box and 240 boxes to a carton.

钢笔10支装一盒,240盒装一纸箱。

2. repack [ri:'pæk] v. to place or arrange (articles) in (a container) again or in a different way 重新包装;改装

3. package ['pækidʒ] n. a collection of things wrapped or boxed together 包件(指包、捆、束、箱等)

e.g. The packages are intact.

包件完整无损。

4. packaging ['pækidʒiŋ] n. material or ways used to make packages 包装方法

e.g. We have improved the packaging.

我们改进了包装方法。

packet ['pækit] n. a small package or bundle 小包(= a small package)

3. Urging Shipment

 (1) Delivery Time is Falling Due

Dear Sirs,

We are very anxious to know about the shipment of our Order No. 123 for 1,000 cases of Tin Plates.

As the contracted time of delivery is rapidly falling due, it is imperative that you inform us of the delivery time without any further delay. We stated explicitly at the outset the importance of punctual execution of this order and cannot help feeling surprised at your silence about our fax inquiry of the June 18th (6 days ago), a copy of which is enclosed.

We are in urgent need of these goods and have to request you to execute the order within the time stipulated.

Yours faithfully,

× × ×

 Notes

1. Tin Plate 锌板
2. fall/ become due 到期

    e.g. The debts of many smaller developers will fall due next year.

    许多更小型开发商的债务将会在明年到期。

3. imperative [im'perətiv] *adj*. if it is imperative that something be done, that thing is extremely important and must be done 绝对必要的；紧急的，迫切的

    e.g. It is imperative that you should ship the goods immediately.

    你方必须立即装运该货。

    e.g. It was imperative that he should act as naturally as possible.

    至关重要的是他要尽可能地自然行事。

4. explicitly [ik'splisitli] *adv*. something that is explicit is expressed or shown clearly and openly, without any attempt to hide anything 清楚地；明确地

    e.g. Therefore, you need to include these in your source files explicitly.

因此，您需要将这些都明确地包含于源文件中。

5. outset ['autset] n. the time at which something is supposed to begin 开端，开始

at/ in the outset 在开头时

from the outset 从一开始

e.g. Decide at the outset what kind of learning programme you want to follow.

一开始就要定下你的学习计划。

e.g. It is such a confident way to open that it establishes attraction from the outset.

正是这种自信的方式开始，它从一开始就确立了吸引力。

 (2) **End Users Need Goods Urgently**

Dear Sirs，

<u>Re：Contract No. W4433</u>

We refer to the above contract signed between us on July 1ˢᵗ, 2018 for 6,000 metric tons of wheat, which is stipulated for shipment in October, 2018. However, up till now we have not received from you any information concerning this lot. As our end users are in urgent need of this material, we intend to send our vessel S.S. "Fengqing" to pick up the goods which is expected to arrive at Vancouver around the end of November. You are requested to let us have your immediate reply by fax whether you are agreeable to this proposal. If not, please let us know exactly the earliest time when the goods will be ready.

We have been put to great inconvenience by the delay in delivery. In case you should fail to effect delivery in November, we will have to lodge a claim against you for the loss and reserve the right to cancel the contract.

Yours faithfully，

×××

 Notes

1. lot [lɒt] n. a batch of goods 一批货物，一批商品

   sell by lots 分批出售

   e.g. We have got a new lot of color TV set for sale.

   我方新到一批彩色电视机出售。

   e.g. You may ship the goods in three lots.

你方可分三批装运此货。

2. pick up（车辆等）中途带（货）

3. reserve [riˈzɜːv] *n*. money kept back or saved for future use or a special purpose 储备，准备金　*vt*. hold back or set aside, especially for future use or contingency 保留

   bank reserve 银行储备金

   foreign exchange reserve 外汇储备

   reserve fund 公积金,储备金

   reserve balance 储备余额

   reserve currency 储备货币

   reserve the right to do sth. 保留做某事的权利

   e.g. He poked around the top of his cabinet for the bottle of whisky that he kept in reserve.

   他在壁橱的上面翻找他留的那瓶威士忌。

   e.g. I reserve the right to disagree.

   我保留持不同意见的权利。

 （3）L/C Will Expire at the End of Next Week

Dear Mr. Wang Jie,

We are now eager to know about the shipment of the racing bicycles as there has not been any news about it from you since the L/C No. 167 was issued two months ago.

By this letter, we wish to call your attention to the fact that the L/C will expire at the end of next week and that we are not going to extend it. This is due to the fact that the distributors and retailers at our end are in urgent need of the goods and we can't afford to wait any more. Therefore we will have to resort to other sources of bicycle suppliers if you fail to make the shipment in the time of validity.

We think that all parties involved would definitely benefit from your prompt action of the shipment. We are looking forward to receiving your shipping advice.

Yours sincerely,

John Smith

 Notes

1. issue [ˈiʃuː; ˈisjuː] *vt./vi.* bring out an official document, come out of 发布；开出

e.g. The government issued a warning that the strikers should end their action or face dismissal.

该政府发出了警告,罢工者们应停止他们的行动,否则将被免职。

e.g. On your appointment you will be issued with a written statement of particulars of employment.

你上任时会收到一份聘用细则的书面材料。

2. call your attention to the fact that 以下情况请你们注意,这种表达法展现了典型的商务英语的风格,行文中起到委婉强调的作用。

e.g. If you do not consider accepting this price, we wish to call your attention to the fact that your competitors will do.

若你方不准备接受此价格,你们的竞争者将会接受。

3. expire [ik'spaiə; ek-] vi. lose validity, to come to an end 期满,过期[信用证上通常会规定有效期,超过这个期限卖方(出口商)即使准确无误地备齐所有单证去银行申请议付,也是会被拒绝的。]

e.g. He had lived illegally in the United States for five years after his visitor's visa expired.

访问签证到期后他在美国非法居住了5年。

e.g. However, most of these contracts expire this month.

不过,这些合同大部分在本月到期。

4. afford [ə'fɔːd] vt. be able to spare or give up or have the financial means to do something or buy something 买得起;给予;提供

afford to do sth. 有经济条件做某事;负担得起某事

can't afford to wait any more 再也等不起了

e.g. We can't afford to wait.

我们等不起。

e.g. My parents can't even afford a new refrigerator.

我父母甚至买不起一台新冰箱。

5. distributor [di'stribjutə] n. someone who markets merchandise 经销商;批发商

6. retailer ['riːteilə] n. a merchant who sells goods at retail 零售商

7. resort to 向……求助

e.g. If other means fail, we shall resort to force.

如果其他手段均失败,我们就将诉诸武力。

e.g. It is better that you resort to yourself than to others.

求人不如求己。

8. in the time of validity 在(信用证)有效期内 【同义】in the valid period; within L/C validity

e.g. You should make the delivery in the time of validity.

你应该在信用证有效期内完成交货。

4. Applying for 3rd Party Inspection

Dear George,

Re: Order No. W153

Referring to the above Order No. W153 for 1,000 screwdriver sets, we are writing this letter to ask your China branch to handle one inspection case for us.

Order No. W153 as attached. DUPRO and final inspection, we need both. I put our supplier's mail in cc line, and she will contact you directly. Thank you.

Best regards,

Eva

 Notes

1. screwdriver ['skru:draivə] n. a hand tool for driving screws; has a tip that fits into the head of a screw 螺丝刀

    screwdriver set 成套螺丝刀

2. handle ['hænd(ə)l] vt. be in charge of, act on, or dispose of 处理；对付；负责某事

    e.g. To tell the truth, I don't know if I can handle the job.

    说实话，我不知道我能否做好这份工作。

3. attach [ə'tætʃ] vt/vi. cause to be attached 附加；使依附

    e.g. It is possible to attach executable program files to email.

    可以在电子邮件上附上可执行程序文件。

    e.g. You can even attach an image to each account.

    你甚至可以在每个帐户上附加一个图像。

4. DUPRO是during production的缩写，意为生产过程中。而DUPRO inspection就是指"产中验货"。当然，也可以用In-line inspection来表达，意思是一样的。如果是完货后的检验，就是final inspection。

5. Shipping Advice

Dear Sirs,

We are pleased to inform you that the following goods under our Contract No. C120 have now been shipped by S. S. "Dongfeng" sailing tomorrow from Guangzhou to Sydney:

    Order NO. C121   10 Bales Grey Cotton Cloth
    Order NO. C122   10 Bales White Cotton Cloth

Copies of the relative shipping documents are enclosed, thus you may find no trouble in taking delivery of the goods when they arrive.

We hope this shipment will reach you in time and turn out to your entire satisfaction.

                                            Best regards,

                                              × × ×

Encl.:   Our Invoice No. 336 in duplicate
          Packing List No. 567 in duplicate
          Non-negotiable Bill of Lading No. 389
          Insurance Policy No. 458
          Survey Report No. FT155

Notes

1. take delivery 提货

    e.g. The buyer must take delivery of the goods when A4 and A7 have been complied with.

    买方必须在卖方按照 A4 和 A7 规定交货时受领货物。

2. invoice ['invɔis] n. an itemized statement of money owed for goods shipped or services rendered 发票

    commercial invoice 商业发票

    e.g. We will then send you an invoice for the total course fees.

    然后我们将寄给你一张全部课程费用的发票。

3. packing list 装箱单
4. non-negotiable bill of lading 不可转让提单
5. insurance policy 保险单
6. survey report 检验报告

Dear Sirs,

We are pleased to have received your L/C No. 98, covering 1,000 dozen "TigerHead" Brand Flashlights under our Sales Confirmation No. TF056 and inform you that shipment was made on S.S. "Dongfeng" on August 3rd for transshipment at HongKong.

Enclosed is a set of the duplicate shipping documents consisting of:
(1) A non-negotiable copy of Bill of Lading;
(2) A Signed Invoice No. 289;
(3) Packing List;
(4) Certificate of Origin No. 1009;
(5) Insurance Policy.

Availing ourselves of this opportunity, we wish to assure you of our cooperation.

We look forward to hearing from you soon.

Yours faithfully,

Liu Hua

 Notes

1. flashlight ['flæʃlait] n. (North American English) a small electric lamp that uses batteries and that you can hold in your hand 手电筒
2. Certificate of Origin 原产地证
3. avail oneself of sth.: to make use of sth., esp. an opportunity or offer 利用(尤指机会、提议等)
    e.g. Guests are encouraged to avail themselves of the full range of hotel facilities.
    旅馆鼓励旅客充分利用各种设施。

Part IV Useful Expressions and Sentences

Expressions

1. do one's endeavour 尽力,竭力
2. with reference to ... 兹谈及
3. packing charges 包装费用
   packing instructions 包装要求,包装须知
   packing list 装箱单
4. fall/ become due 到期
5. at/ in the outset 在开头时
   from the outset 从一开始
6. sell by lots 分批出售
7. pick up (车辆等)中途带(货)
8. reserve the right to do sth. 保留做某事的权利
9. bank reserve 银行储备金
   foreign exchange reserve 外汇储备
   reserve fund 公积金,储备金
   reserve balance 储备余额
   reserve currency 储备货币
10. DUPRO/ In-line inspection 产中验货
    final inspection 完货后的检验
11. distributor 经销商,批发商
12. retailer 零售商
13. resort to 向某某求助
14. take delivery 提货
15. commercial invoice 商业发票
16. packing list 装箱单
17. non-negotiable bill of lading 不可转让提单
18. insurance policy 保险单
19. survey report 检验报告
20. call your attention to the fact that 以下情况请你们注意

Typical Sentences

1. We have been put to considerable inconvenience by the long delay in delivery.

We must insist on immediate delivery, otherwise we shall be compelled to cancel the orders in accordance with the stipulations of the contract.

2. It is important that the goods be completed for delivery as stipulated in the L/C, say by October 20th. If not, you should be responsible for any loss that might be caused by the delay of shipment.

3. For the goods under our Contract No. SC456 we have booked space on S. S. "East Wind" due to arrive in Sydney around May 19th. Please communicate with B & W Bros. Co. Singapore, our shipping agents, for loading arrangements.

4. We shall be glad to know the time of transit and frequency of sailing, and whether cargo space must be reserved. If so, please send us the necessary application forms.

5. The goods have been packed and marked exactly as directed so that they may be shipped by the first ship available towards the end of this month.

6. We shall ship the goods in three monthly installments for 500 tons as stipulated in the contract, commencing in August.

7. The goods will be forwarded to you within the 2nd quarter of the year.

8. Please book the necessary shipping space in advance to ensure timely dispatch of the goods ordered.

9. According to the terms of Contract No. 308, shipment is to be effected by January 20th, and we must have the B/L by the 31st at the latest.

10. We are pleased to inform you that the goods under your Order No. 103 were shipped by the direct steamer "Red Sun" on November 30th, and the relevant shipping samples had been dispatched to you by air before the steamer sailed.

Part Ⅴ Practical Training

Ⅰ. Elementary Training

1. Choose the best answer.

(1) Goods will be shipped ____ 30 days after receipt of the L/C.

 A. to   B. on   C. for   D. within

(2) Direct steamers to your port are few ____ the winter season.

 A. but   B. yet   C. with   D. during

(3) The goods will be shipped ____ October 1st.

A. in		B. to		C. on		D. with

(4) Please note that Item No. 1-10 can be certainly promised for immediate shipment ____ receipt of your order.

A. if		B. whether		C. upon		D. at

(5) We suggest that you file a claim ____ the shipping company for all the losses incurred as a consequence of the failure to ship the goods ____ Order T211 in time.

A. against, unless		B. for, under
C. to, in		D. against, under

(6) We make it clear ____ shipment will be effected in August.

A. what		B. that		C. which		D. when

(7) We regret the delayed delivery and the inconvenience ____ it is causing you.

A. /		B. that		C. which		D. what

(8) We will do our best to ____ shipment to meet your requirements in time.

A. comply		B. make		C. expedite		D. arrange

(9) The shipment time is June or July at our ____ and the goods will be shipped in one ____.

A. choice, shipment		B. option, lot
C. decision, cargo		D. option, consignment

(10) We regret our inability to ____ with your request for shipping the goods in early November.

A. compliance		B. comply		C. manage		D. arrange

(11) They intended to lower the cost of the products. ____ they didn't succeed in reducing the package costs.

A. Therefore		B. And		C. However		D. Furthermore

(12) I wonder if you could advance the shipment by one month ____ we need it badly.

A. provided		B. as		C. or		D. because of

2. Read the following letters and fill in each blank with prepositions.

Letter 1

Dear Mr. Nixon,

Re: Order No. 217 for 1,000 M/T Tin Foil Sheets

Referring ___(1)___ our letters ___(2)___ respect ___(3)___ Order No. 217 for 1,000 metric tons of Tin Foil Sheets, so far we have no definite information __(4)__ you about delivery time, although these goods are contracted __(5)__ shipment before the end of last month, and our relative L/C was opened with the Bank of China as early as in March, 2018.

Needless __(6)__ say, we have been inconvenienced __(7)__ the delay. It's therefore imperative that you notify us immediately of the earliest possible date of shipment __(8)__ our consideration.

Please look up the matter and give us your definite reply without further delay.

Yours faithfully,

×××

Letter 2

Dear Sirs,

Re: Contract No. 633

Referring to our previous letters and cables, we wish __(1)__ call your attention __(2)__ the fact that up __(3)__ the present moment no news has come from you __(4)__ the shipment under the captioned contract.

As you have been informed in one of our previous letters, the users are __(5)__ need of the goods contracted and are in fact pressing us for assurance __(6)__ timely delivery. __(7)__ the circumstances, we are obliged __(8)__ remind you of this matter once again.

As your prompt attention to shipment is most desirable __(9)__ all parties concerned, we hope you will let us have your shipping advice by fax without fail.

Yours faithfully,

×××

3. Translate the following English into Chinese.

(1) shipping mark

(2) inner packing

(3) port of shipment

(4) port of destination

(5) partial shipment

(6) marine transport/ocean transport

(7) transshipment

(8) The goods are to be shipped in three lots of 20 tons each on separate bills of lading.

(9) The above order is now ready for shipment. Please give us your shipping instructions as soon as possible.

(10) As the market is sluggish, please postpone the shipment of our ordered goods to March.

(11) If you desire earlier shipment, we can only make a partial shipment of 50 tons in July and the balance of 50 tons in August.

(12) Please book the shipping space immediately with COSCO under advice to us.

(13) As direct sailing to your port from here few and far between, we hope that partial shipments are allowed to make it easier for us to get the goods ready for shipment.

(14) You must make shipment before the end of October without fail, otherwise we will not be able to catch the season.

(15) We have pleasure in informing you that the cargo has been shipped on S. S. "Dongfeng" for transshipment at Hongkong onto S. S. "Manhattan", and we hope that it will arrive at the destination in perfect condition.

II. Intermediate Training

1. Supply the missing words in the blanks of the following letter. The first letters are given.

Dear Sir or Madam,

We are pleased to a_____ you that above order has now been dispatched.

The electrical drills are in fifty separate crates marked ED MANILA and numbered 1 to 100. The c_____ is on the M. V. Mermaid, which l_____ Shanghai on June 21st, and is d_____ in Manila on July 2nd.

We have p____ to the Overseas Chinese Banking Corporation our draft for the amount of your L/C t____ with a full set of shipping d____ consisting of clean, shipped on board Bill of Lading in triplicate. Certificate of Insurance, Certificate of Origin and our invoice in triplicate.

We hope that the drills will p____ suitable for your customers' needs and look f____ to receiving your next order.

Sincerely yours,

×××

2. Cloze. Choose the most suitable words from the list of words to fill in the blanks. Each word can be used only once.

draw   inform   pass   arrive   order   present   leave

Dear Sirs,

Re: Your Order No.678

We are pleased to __(1)__ you that arrangements have now been made to ship the sewing machines you __(2)__ on November 11th last year. The consignments will __(3)__ Shanghai by S.S. Dongfeng, due to __(4)__ at Port Kelang sometime in late January.

In keep with our usual terms of payment we __(5)__ on you at 60 days and __(6)__ the draft and shipping documents to our bank. The documents will be __(7)__ to you by the Chartered Bank against your acceptance of the draft in the usual way.

Yours faithfully,

×××

3. Translate the following Chinese into English.

(1) 发货人

(2) 收货人

(3) 承运人

(4) 装船须知

(5) 装箱单

(6) 保险单

(7) 重量单

(8) 原产地证明

(9) 商业发票

(10) 提单

(11) 装船通知

(12) 装船日期

(13) 装货港

(14) 剩余货物将在 11 月上旬装船。

(15) 我们一收到信用证就安排装船。

(16) 必须赶在 8 月交货,否则赶不上季节。

(17) 由于圣诞节销售旺季即将来临,买主催促我们立即交货,否则他们就赶不上季节。

(18) 我们可以分批装运,也就是说,50% 在 9 月交货,剩余的在 10 月交货。

(19) 合同规定需分两批等量装运。

(20) 每件衬衫装一个塑料袋,20 件装一盒。

Ⅲ. Advanced Training

1. Translate the following letter into English.

收到你方 789 号信用证,谢谢。经核对条款,我们遗憾地发现你方信用证要求 2019 年 10 月装运,但我方合约规定 11 月装运。因此,务请把装运期和议付期分别延展至 2019 年 11 月 30 日和 12 月 15 日。请即办理展证事宜,并尽早电复。

2. Letter composing: compose a letter on behalf of Mr. Liu Bao, sales manager of Export Department, according to the given message, telling Mr. H. J. Wilkinson, the sales manager, the shipment about the order. Then arrange the necessary parts in proper form as they should be set out in a business letter.

Message:

(1) 告诉对方 876 号订单项下的 1,000 台冰箱已于今天下午在广州装船起运。

(2) 我方会于明天把有关运输单据传真给对方,单据正本会通过议付行及开证行交给对方。

(3) 这一整套单据均为信用证中所要求的提供的,包括海运提单、保险单、商业发票、装箱单以及原产地证等。

(4) 对于对方未来订单,我方将一如既往地迅速处理、周到服务。

Unit 8　Insurance
保　　险

☙ Lead-in ☙

Try to finish the following tasks and find out the learning objectives of this unit.

Task 1

　　假设你是美国富兰克林公司的经理,不久前,你公司和上海纺织品进出口公司达成了一宗在 CFR 条件下向其订购 5,000 打毛衣的交易。为方便起见,上海方面可以为你们代办保险。现在,请代表你们公司致函该公司,向其说明情况并提出你们的要求。注意信中包含以下内容:

　　(1) 关于我方向贵公司订购 5,000 打毛衣一事,我方已经通过美国花旗银行开出了以你方为受益人的即期信用证。你们可以放心备货了。

　　(2) 另有一件事相商:由于我们的协议是在 CFR 的条件下达成的,保险本应由我方办理,但为了方便起见,能否请贵方替我们代办呢?

　　(3) 若无异议,请在当地替我们按发票金额的 110% 为合同项下的货物投保水渍险和偷窃及提货不着险。

　　(4) 所有的保险费用由我们承担。贵方完成投保手续后可向我方开出即期汇票收取该费用。

Task 2

　　假设你是上海纺织品进出口公司的销售经理,接到上述信件并权衡各方面因素之后,你认为你们公司可以为美国公司代办保险。现在,请致函中国人民保险公司上海分公司向其询问投保手续及保险费率的问题。注意信中务必包含以下内容:

　　(1) 我们是上海主要的纺织品出口商,下个月将要向美国波士顿出口两个货柜的毛衣。

　　(2) 知道贵公司经营海洋货物运输保险业务,我方有意按发票金额的 110% 对这批价值

150万美元的货物向贵公司投保水渍险和偷窃及提货不着险。

（3）投保范围是从我方仓库到美国麻省波士顿港口。请报最优惠保险费率。

Part Ⅰ Introduction

在国际贸易中，货物可能会遇到各种各样的危险，并遭受损失。为了保护这些货物，卖家或者买家会在货物运输前向保险公司进行投保。保险的目的是为遭受损失或损害的人提供赔偿。这是一份赔偿合同，通常是以保险单的形式订立。

通常情况下有三种基本险别，分别是平安险、水渍险和一切险，投保人可以选择其中的一种进行投保。就风险范围而言，平安险包含在水渍险中，水渍险包含在一切险中。

另外还有 11 种附加险分别是：（1）偷窃及提货不着险；（2）淡水雨淋险；（3）短量险；（4）混杂玷污险；（5）渗漏险；（6）碰损破碎险；（7）串味险；（8）受潮受热险；（9）钩损险；（10）包装破裂险；（11）锈损险。附加险不能单独投保，可在投保一种基本险的基础上，根据货运需要加保其中的一种或若干种。投保了一切险后，因一切险中已包括了所有一般附加险的责任范围，所以只需在特殊附加险中选择加保。

特殊附加险有战争险、罢工险、交货不到险、进口关税险、舱面险、拒收险、黄曲霉素险和货物出口到香港（包括九龙）或澳门存仓火险责任扩展条款等。

Part Ⅱ Letter Writing Guide

1. For letters from the importer requesting the exporter to insure the goods 进口商要求出口商办理保险

（1）Referring to which shipment of goods is to be insured against.

（2）Stating the risks coverage to insure against and the amount of the insured value.

（3）Clarifying the payment of the premium.

（4）Expressing your expectation.

2. For letters in reply 回复函电

（1）Confirming the receipt of the importer's request.

（2）Informing the importer of what has been done.

（3）Clarifying the payment of the premium charge.

Part III Sample Letters

1. Importer Asks Exporter to Cover Insurance

Dear Sirs,

We wish to refer to our Order No. 12 for 1,000 sets of TCL Color Television, from which you will see that this order is placed on a CFR basis.

In order to save time and simplify procedures, we now desire to have the shipment insured at your end. We shall be pleased if you will arrange to insure the goods on our behalf against All Risks for 110% of the invoice value, i. e., US$ 100,000. May we suggest that you would follow our proposal.

We shall of course refund you the premium upon receipt of your debit note or, if you like, you may draw on us at sight for the amount required.

We sincerely hope that our request will meet your approval.

Yours faithfully,

×××

 Notes

1. cover insurance 投保,办保险 【同义】arrange insurance; effect insurance
2. refer to our Order No. 123 请你查看一下我方第 123 号订单
    refer sb. to sth. 请某人查看某物/事,使(某人)向……咨询
    e.g. They refer us to your company for information.
    他们让我们向贵公司咨询有关信息。
3. at your end 你处,你地
4. on our behalf 代表我方
5. for 110% of the invoice value 按发票金额的 110%
6. refund you the premium 将保险费偿付给你方
7. debit note 索款通知

8. draw on us at sight for the amount required 开即期汇票向我们收取所需金额

2. Exporter's Response of Having Covered Insurance

Dear Sirs,

      Re: Your Order No. 123 for 1,000 sets of TCL Color Television

We have received your letter requesting us to effect insurance on the captioned shipment for your account. We are pleased to inform you that we have covered the above shipment against All Risks for US$ 100,000 with the People's Insurance Company of China, which is a state-operated enterprise enjoying high prestige in settling claims promptly and equitably. The policy is being prepared accordingly and will be forwarded to you by the end of the week together with our debit note for the premium.

For your reference, we are making arrangements to ship the 1,000 sets of TCL Color Television from Shanghai to New York, by S. S. "Princess", sailing on or about the 15th of July.

Yours faithfully,

×××

 Notes

1. the captioned shipment 标题货物
2. for your account 由你方承担
3. the People's Insurance Company of China 中国人民保险公司
4. which is a state-operated enterprise enjoying high prestige in settling claims promptly and equitably
   中国人民保险公司是国有企业,享有理赔迅速、处理公平的声誉
5. forwarded to you 被提交给你方

3. The Insured Asking for Information About Insurance

Dear Sirs,

We are a Guangzhou-based import & export company and going to ship 10 containers of household electrical appliances to Rome next week. We want to insure the goods with you, who we know has a prestigious position in the insurance industry, if the rate is within our expectation.

Would you please quote us your most favorable premium rate of the said goods for the insured value of US$ 150,000 against All Risks plus War Risk? The insurance coverage is from our warehouse to the port of Rome.

We are awaiting your information.

Yours faithfully,

×××

Notes

1. Guangzhou-based 总部设在广州的
2. electrical appliances 家用电器;电器用具

4. Reply to the Letter of the Above

Dear Mr. Beare,

We acknowledge the receipt of your letter inquiring about the rate of your household appliances exported to Rome.

The premium for the above-mentioned goods is at the rate of 0.8% of the insured value declared against All Risks plus 0.4% against War Risk. You will find it most favorable among the market-leading insurers.

If the rate is acceptable to you, please let us know at your earliest convenience so that we could prepare and send the policy to you in due course.

Yours faithfully,

×××

Notes

1. The premium for the above-mentioned goods is at the rate of 0.8% of the insured value

declared against All Risks plus 0.4% against War Risk.

上述商品投保一切险的费率为保险金额的0.8%,加投战争险的费率为保险金额的0.4%。

2. market-leading 在市场上占主导地位的

Part IV　Useful Expressions and Sentences

Expressions

1. insurance company; the insurer; underwriter 保险公司;承保人,保险人

2. the insured 被保险人,受益人

3. insurance policy 保险单

4. insurance certificate 保险凭证,简式保单,小保单

5. open policy 预约保单,总保单

6. insurance amount/ value 保险金额

7. insurance premium 保险费

   premium rate 保险费率

8. insurance agent 保险经纪人

9. insurance coverage 保险范围(指险别或金额范围)

10. Free from Particular Average (FPA) 平安险
    With Particular Average (WPA/ WA) 水渍险

11. General Additional Risk 一般附加险

12. Special Additional Risk 特殊附加险

13. Fresh Water &/ or Rain Damage (FWRD) 淡水雨淋险

14. intermixture & contamination 混杂玷污险

15. Risk of Clash & Breakage 碰损破碎险

16. with a franchise of ...% 有一个……%的免赔率

17. cover/ effect/ arrange/ take out/ attend to/ provide/ handle insurance 投保,办保险

    insure ...(goods) against ...(risk) for ...(value) 按……金额为……商品投保……险

    cover ...(goods) against ...(risk) 为……货物投保……险

18. insure ... with ...(insurance company) 向……保险公司投保……货物

Typical Sentences

1. Please see that the above mentioned goods should be covered for 150% of invoice

value against All Risks. We know that according to your usual practice, you insure the goods only for 10% above invoice value; therefore the extra premium will be for our account.

2. In the absence of definite instructions from our clients, we generally cover insurance against W.P.A. and War Risk; if you desire to cover F.P.A., please let us know in advance.

3. If you wish to secure protection against T.P.N.D., it can be easily done upon the payment of an additional premium.

4. We are making regular shipments from Shanghai to New York and should be glad to hear whether you would be prepared to issue an open policy.

5. According to our usual practice we prefer our export shipment to be insured by the People's Insurance Company of China.

6. Before completing the shipment we will insure the consignment with the local branch of the PICC as per the risks coverage and insured value you mentioned.

7. It has become the common sense that the insurance of goods traded on the basis of CFR or FOB terms is supposed to be arranged by the buyer.

8. Owing to the risk of war, we cannot accept the insurance at the ordinary rate. At the same time, it would be to your advantage to have particular average cover.

9. For transactions concluded on CIF basis, we usually cover the insurance against All Risks at invoice value plus 10% with the People's Insurance Company of China as per CIC of January 1st, 1981.

10. For the sake of convenience, we wonder whether you could have the goods insured, on behalf of us, against All Risks, Breakage and War Risk for 110% of the invoice value at your end.

Part V Practical Training

I. Elementary Training

1. Choose the best answer.

(1) Since three fifths of the voyage is in tropical weather and the goods are liable to go mouldy, we think it advisable to have the shipment ____ the risk of mould.

    A. covered insurance   B. taken out insured

    C. covered against   D. insured for

(2) The insurance certification is being prepared accordingly and ____ to you by the end of this week.
　　A. will be forwarded　　　　B. will forward
　　C. will send　　　　　　　　D. will be passed

(3) The extra premium ____ by us.
　　A. is born　　　　　　　　　B. will be taken
　　C. will be borne　　　　　　D. will be undertaken

(4) We enclose an inspection certificate ____ by the Shanghai Commodity Inspection Bureau.
　　A. issued　　B. to be issued　　C. being issued　　D. having been issued

(5) In the absence of your definite instructions ____ insurance, we covered your goods against W.P.A.
　　A. concerning　　B. regarding　　C. referring　　D. against

(6) If you desire to ____ your goods against All Risks, we can provide such coverage.
　　A. guarantee　　B. guard　　C. cover　　D. protect

(7) Should any damage ____, you may file your claim.
　　A. incur　　B. incurred　　C. incurring　　D. be incurred

(8) We will effect insurance ____ All Risks as requested.
　　A. for　　B. against　　C. by　　D. with

(9) We shall be pleased if you will arrange to insure the goods ____ our behalf ____ invoice value plus 10%.
　　A. on; at　　B. to; at　　C. to; with　　D. on; with

(10) Please give us the policy rate ____ F.P.A. coverage.
　　A. with　　B. in　　C. of　　D. to

2. Read the following letters and fill in each black with prepositions.

Letter 1

Dear Sirs,

　　We wish to insure the following leather shoes __(1)__ the PICC __(2)__ WPA including TPND and FWRD __(3)__ the amount of US$ 3,000.

　　These goods are now lying __(4)__ Deck No.3 Huangpu Port of Guangzhou, waiting to be shipped __(5)__ S.S. Morning Star due to sail for Antwerp(安特卫普,荷兰港口) tomorrow morning.

Could you cover the insurance for the above goods, on our behalf, with Guangzhou Branch of the PICC immediately?

Yours faithfully,

× × ×

Letter 2

Dear Sirs,

This is to acknowledge the receipt __(1)__ your letter asking us to cover the leather shoes __(2)__ Guangzhou __(3)__ Antwerp on behalf of you.

We have gone through all the insurance procedures with the PICC Guangzhou Branch. The premium is __(4)__ the rate of 0.8% of the declared value against the risks you demanded. The insurer is preparing the policy and will send to you __(5)__ one day or two. And they have confirmed that the consignment is held covered as from today.

Yours faithfully,

× × ×

 3. **Translate the following English into Chinese.**

(1) cover insurance

(2) the captioned shipment

(3) at your end

(4) for our account

(5) handle insurance business

(6) insurance rate

(7) insurance contracts

(8) the insurer

(9) issue an insurance policy

(10) the premium

(11) Please insure the following goods against all risks plus war risk.

(12) Please effect the following insurance against T.P.N.D.

(13) The additional premium is for the buyer's account.

(14) We have enclosed the insurance policy so that you can lodge a claim with the insurer's branch office at the destination port in due course should any damage or loss be found when you receive the goods.

(15) Insurance should be arranged by the seller in the CIF trade term.

(16) The insurance must be covered for the amount of invoice value plus 15%.

(17) We request you to extend the insurance coverage to include Risk of Breakage.

(18) Should the loss or damage be incurred, you might, within 60 days after the arrival of the shipment, lodge a claim with the insurer.

(19) According to our usual practice we prefer our export shipment to be insured by the People's Insurance Company of China.

(20) I'd like to have the insurance of the goods covered at 130% of the invoice amount.

II. Intermediate Training

1. Supply the missing words in the blanks of the following letter. The first letters are given.

Dear Sirs,

In reply, we would like to i____ you that most of our clients are p____ their orders with us on CIF b____. This will s____ their time and s____ procedures. May we suggest that you would f____ this practice?

For your i____, we usually e____ insurance with the People's Insurance Company of China for 110% of the invoice value. Our insurance company is a s____ enterprise enjoying high p____ in s____ claims promptly and e____ and has agents at all main ports and regions of the world.

We hope that you will a____ to our s____ and look forward to your favorable reply.

Yours faithfully,

×××

2. Cloze. Choose the most suitable words form the list of words to fill in the blanks. Each word can be used only once.

consignment   fragile   Breakage   insurer   insured
rate   insure   packing   coverage   advice

Dear Sirs,

Thank you for your letter of August 20th, informing us that you are ready to __(1)__ 500 cartons of coffee mugs against All Risks and __(2)__.

As we know the __(3)__ goods such as glassware and chinaware is __(4)__ against the risk of breakage at a __(5)__ as high as 5% of the insured value. And __(6)__ does not accept claims for loss less than 5% of the entire __(7)__. Therefore occasional minor breakage which possibly occurs will not be compensated for. In my opinion serious breakage can doubtlessly be avoided so long as special care is given to the __(8)__ and handling of the goods. We believe that the __(9)__ of All Risks is enough.

Thank you anyway for bringing up the matter to our consideration and we are looking forward to receiving your shipping __(10)__ timely.

Yours faithfully,

×××

3. Translate the following Chinese into English.
(1) 代表我方
(2) 提前
(3) 投保
(4) 按照你方指示
(5) 保险范围
(6) 特惠保率
(7) 中国人民保险公司
(8) 发票金额
(9) 一切险
(10) 一般附加险

(11) 为了您的利益,可以进行单独海损的保险。

(12) 根据你方要求,我们将按发票金额的110%投保。

(13) 我们很高兴地通知你们,我们已向中国人民保险公司为上述货物投保了战争险。

(14) 给货物投保时须在平安险、水渍险及一切险这三种基本险中选择一种。

(15) 我方按惯例将以发票金额的110%为这批出口丝绸衬衣投保一切险和战争险。

(16) 在CIF条件下我们通常以发票金额的110%为买方投保水渍险,假设买方想增加保险金额或扩大保险范围,则超出部分的保险费由其本人承担。

(17) 我们将把保险单连同保险费的借记通知邮寄给你们。

(18) 这种险别的保险费是按你方所申报价值十万美元的2.3%计算的。

(19) 我们已按发票金额的110%为100公吨羊毛向中国人民保险公司投保一切险,保险费率为3%。

(20) 碰损破碎险是一种一般附加险。

Ⅲ. Advanced Training

 1. Translate the following letter into English.

敬启者:

请开出150,000英镑的保险单,包含从广州装船、到达伦敦港口的1,000台松下电冰箱的一切险费用。

由于装船是10月1号开始,请即刻提供给我们贵方的报价。

 2. Write a letter from the following particulars.

(1) Write to the exporter-Chinese National Import & Export Corporation. Ask him to cover insurance on your behalf.

(2) You import 500 sets of "Xingqiu" Band radio from the exporter on CFR basis, the value is US$ 5,000. The consignment will be shipped from Tianjin to New York on or about January 10th.

(3) Tell the exporter to cover the insurance against All Risks for 110% of the invoice value.

(4) The insurance charges will be borne by you.

Module 6
The Receipt of Payment by the Seller
卖方收款

Unit 9 Payment
支 付

Lead-in

Try to finish the following tasks and find out the learning objectives of this unit.

Task 1

假设你是上海纺织品进出口有限公司的外贸业务员李林,你与美国一公司达成了一笔关于棉布的交易。按照约定,对方在下订单时已经支付了70%的货款。货物装船后,请对方支付剩余的货款。注意信中包括以下内容:

(1) AB112号订单项下的印花棉布已经装上东风号,预计在3月10号到达你方港口。

(2) 请对方立即按照约定电汇剩余的20,000美金。

(3) 收到货款后会立即电放提单。

(4) 感谢对方的配合。

Task 2

假设你是美国一纺织品经销商,和上海纺织品进出口有限公司达成了关于棉布的交易。收到信后,已经按照要求安排银行付款,并附上水单。

注意信中包含以下内容:

(1) 非常高兴得知AB112号订单下的印花棉布已经装上船。

(2) 按照卖方要求,已经通知银行电汇20,000美金尾款。

(3) 附上银行水单,请卖家查收。

(4) 希望今后可以有更多、更广泛的合作。

Part I Introduction

外贸业务中,常见的支付方式有三种,汇付、托收和信用证。

1. 汇付(Remittance)

汇付分为电汇(T/T,Telegraphic Transfer)、信汇(M/T,Mail Transfer)和票汇(D/D,Demand Draft),其中电汇最常用。

电汇根据客户付款时间的不同又可分为以下几种类型:

(1) 下单后即付清全部货款

对外贸企业来说,这是最安全的一种收款方式,一般适用于数量较小的订单,或是市场上供不应求的商品。

(2) 下单后先付定金,出货后客户见提单资料付清尾款

这是国际贸易中常用的一种收款方式,外贸企业只有在收到客户尾款后,才会申请提单电放,确保货款安全。

(3) 下单后先付定金,但尾款有账期,譬如:合同约定尾款在开船后两个月付清

这种收款方式对外贸企业有很大的风险,事先必须对客户的信用状况进行充分了解。

(4) 下单后不付定金,且尾款有账期,譬如:合同约定尾款在开船后两个月付清

这种收款方式是风险最大的,但现在确实有很多客户就是采用这种付款方式。

(5) 其他付款组合

参照上述付款方式,结合实际情况的不同,还有其他付款组合。对于金额较大的合同,定金可能会分几次支付(譬如:签订合同时支付10%,生产开工时再支付20%);尾款的账期也会分几次支付(譬如:开船后两个月支付50%,三个月支付20%);有的合同还会约定一定比例的质保金(譬如:六个月后付清5%的质保金)。

对于信用状况相对较好的客户,大多采用电汇的收款方式。电汇不仅操作方便、收款速度快,而且手续费也比信用证要低很多。

2. 托收(Collection)

托收是指在进出口贸易中,出口方开具以进口方为付款人的汇票,委托出口方银行通过其在进口方的分行或代理行向进口方收取货款的一种结算方式。托收包括付款交单(D/P,Documents against Payment)和承兑交单(D/A,Documents against Acceptance)。

托收属于商业信用,银行办理托收业务时,既没有检查货运单据正确与否或是否完整的义务,也没有承担付款人必须付款的责任。托收虽然是通过银行办理,但银行只是作为出口

人的受托人行事,并没有承担付款的责任,进口方不付款与银行无关。托收对出口方的风险较大,D/A比D/P的风险更大。

3. 信用证(L/C)

对于其他信用状况不是很好的国外客户,为确保资金安全,一般采用信用证的收款方式。

(1) 不可撤销信用证

信用证根据是否可以撤销,分为可撤销信用证和不可撤销信用证两类,外贸企业必须要求客户开具不可撤销的信用证。

(2) 即期信用证

信用证根据付款时间的不同,分为即期信用证和远期信用证。为了及时收回货款,外贸企业应尽量要求客户开具即期信用证。

(3) 注意不符点

大多数客户开具的信用证,内容都比较简单,交单的时候不符点相对较少;但是也有一些比较苛刻的客户,会在信用证上罗列很多要求。在操作的时候需要特别注意,业务和单证、财务一定要相互配合,以免出现过多的不符点而被扣款。

(4) 信用证保险

出口信用保险可以为外贸企业保驾护航,是国际贸易中确保出口企业资金安全的一道有力的屏障。中国出口信用保险公司可以通过其遍布全球的网络,帮助外贸企业规避收款风险,尤其是对于合同金额较大、信用状况不是很好的客户,信用证保险可以确保外贸企业的资金安全。中信保拒绝提供保险的信用证,这样的客户有很大的收款风险但是如果遇到外贸企业一定要慎重对待。

电汇和信用证有时候也可以结合起来使用,譬如付定金的时候用电汇,尾款则通过信用证结算,这种收款方式也是较为安全的。

除了以上三种常见的支付方式以外,为了操作方便,有些规模不大的外贸企业、外贸SOHO也会采用其他的一些收款方式,如离岸账户、国内银行私人账户、西联汇款、PayPal等,但不管哪种收款方式,都各有利弊。最重要的是,这些支付方式都是在国家外汇管理局的严格监管之下,外贸企业也需要遵守国家的外汇规定。严格遵守海关、税务、银行的各项规定,是外贸企业健康发展的必由之路。

Part Ⅱ Letter Writing Guide

1. For letters pushing payment 催款函

(1) Referring to the goods, relative order and the shipment.

(2) Urging the buyer to make payment, stating the money and payment terms.

(3) Expressing your gratitude.

2. For letters receiving the payment made from customer 收到客户付款通知

(1) Notifying the payment has been made.

(2) Enclosing bank receipt if any.

(3) Requesting for origins of documents and telex release.

3. For letters asking for bank receipt 请客户提供银行汇款凭证

(1) Referring to the goods, relative order or the shipment.

(2) Asking for the bank receipt and stating the reason.

(3) Expressing your gratitude.

4. For letters discussing payment errors 发现付款错误跟客户重新谈论

(1) Stating the payment errors.

(2) Asking for re-checking.

(3) Proposing the settlement.

5. For letters informing of receiving payment 告知客户款项收到

(1) Referring to the goods, relative order number or contract.

(2) Stating that payment has been received.

(3) Expressing your expectation for further business.

6. For letters proposing acceptation of L/C discrepancies 请客户接受信用证不符点

(1) Stating the discrepancies and the reason causing these discrepancies.

(2) Requesting the buyers to tell the bank that they have accepted these discrepancies.

(3) Expressing your gratitude.

7. For letters proposing new payment terms of order 讨论新订单付款方式

(1) Expressing your satisfaction of the fact that business have been done.

(2) Asking for new payment terms.

(3) Stating the reason why you asking for new payment terms.

(4) Expecting agreement and expressing your gratitude in advance.

Part Ⅲ Sample Letters

1. Documentary Submission and Payment Push

Dear Mr. White,

We have shipped your order No. 123 on board s.s. "Victory" last Wednesday.

Enclosed please find the commercial invoice, packing list and a copy of B/L.

The vessel is due to leave Shanghai for Hamburg on July 6th.

Please help to settle the rest payment USD 5,000 to our bank account soon.

Thanks a lot.

Yours sincerely,

×××

 Notes

1. board [bɔːd] *n./v.* 甲板；上（飞机、车、船等）

   on board 在船（火车、飞机）上

   e.g. The cargo on board has been damaged by sea water.

   船上的货物被海水浸湿而受损。

2. enclosed please find 随函寄去……，请查收

   e.g. Enclosed please find our sales confirmation in duplicate.

   随函寄去销售确认书一式两份，请查收。

3. packing list 装箱单

   e.g. Packing list is a document which details the contents, dimensions and weight of each package.

   装箱单是详细说明每件包装的货物名称、尺寸和重量的文件。

4. B/L bill of lading 提单，是指用以证明海上货物运输合同和货物已经由承运人接收或者装船，以及承运人保证据以交付货物的单证。

5. be due to 定于某时做某事，在这儿表示轮船、飞机等交通工具按照时刻表出发或者到达。

   e.g. The plane is due to leave at 9 a.m. 飞机预计上午九点起飞。

6. settle ['setl] *v.* 付清（欠款）；结算；结账

   settle sth./ settle (up) (with sb.): to pay the money that you owe

   e.g. The insurance company is refusing to settle her claim.

   保险公司拒付她提出的索赔款项。

   e.g. Please settle your bill before leaving the hotel.

   请您离开旅馆前先结账。

2. Receiving the Payment Advice Made from Customer

Dear Wang Qiang,

We have transferred the balance of USD 5,000. Please check the bank receipt in attachment.

Telex release is acceptable to us. There is no need to send us the original documents.

Yours sincerely,

×××

Notes

1. transfer [træsˈfɜː] v. move money from one account or institution to another 把(钱)转到另一账户(机构)上

   e.g. I'd like to transfer $500 to my checking account.

   我想转 500 美元到我的活期账户上。

2. balance [ˈbæləns] n. the balance of a debt is the amount of money you still owe after you have paid some of it (债务的)余款 the amount of money that you have in your bank account 账户余额;结余

   e.g. The balance is due at the end of next month.

   余款需要在下个月底支付。

   e.g. My bank balance isn't good.

   我银行账户里的余额不多了。

   余款的其他表示方式：rest payment; outstanding money

   e.g. Tom asked whether we had arranged the rest payment.

   汤姆问我们是否已经付了余款。

   e.g. Please help to settle the outstanding money to our bank account.

   请帮忙把剩余的钱转到我方的银行账户。

3. receipt [rɪˈsiːt] n. a piece of paper that you are given which shows that you have paid for something 收据

   e.g. I wrote her a receipt for the money of USD 500.

   这笔 500 美金的钱我给她开了收据。

4. attachment [əˈtætʃmənt] n. a document of file that is sent with an email message(电子邮件的)附件

e.g. I'll send the spreadsheet as an attachment.

我将把电子表格作为附件发送。

5. telex release 提单电放（通过电子报文或者电子信息形式把提单信息发送至目的港船公司，收货人可凭加盖电放章的提单电放件和电放保函进行换单提货。）

电放提单指船公司或其代理人签发的注有"电放"（Surrendered, Telex Release）字样的提单。基本流程为供应商通知货代提交电放申请单或者出具保函，然后货代通知船公司安排电放。需要注意的是提货人电放提单的真正含义是放弃领取提单的权利。也就是说，从电放的那一刻起，货权就不再由自己掌握，提货人仅仅依靠提单复印件就可以在卸货港提货。

6. original [əˈridʒənl] n. a work of art or a document that is not a copy, but is the one produced by the writer or artist（艺术作品或文件的）原作；原稿；原件 adj. painted, written, etc. by the artist rather than copied 原作的；原件的

e.g. I'll keep a copy of the contract, and give you the original.

我留一份合同副本，把原件给你。

original documents 单据正本

e.g. Only original documents will be accepted as proof of status.

只有文件正本才能用做身份证明。

3. Asking for Banking Receipt

Dear Mr. Woods,

We regret to inform you/kindly be noted that your balance of USD 5,000 has not been received yet.

Could you kindly re-check it and send the bank receipt to us for our record.

Thank you for your cooperation!

Yours sincerely,

×××

 Notes

1. regret [riˈgret] v. used in official letters or statements when saying that you are sorry or sad about something 对……感到抱歉或遗憾（用于正式的函电或声明中）

We regret to say/inform/tell sb. that ...

e.g. I regret to inform you that our contract will not be renewed.

我很遗憾地通知你,你的合同将不予续签。

2. re-check 再核对;再检查

e.g. Before you hit "send", take a moment to recheck the details of your email.

在点击发送之前,请再核对一下邮件中的细节。

3. for our record 便于我方备案

e.g. Please sign and return one copy for our record.

还有一种说法 for one's file 供某人存档

4. Re-discussion for Payment Error

Dear Steve,

We were informed from our bank that our account was added by USD 1,000 as wire transfer.

I think the money belongs to other suppliers of yours. Is it possible to return the money by check or other way?

Please let us know if you have any difficult in making the payment.

We look forward to your early reply.

Yours sincerely,

×××

 Notes

1. wire transfer 电汇

    Wire transfer 是一种资金转账方式,常用于不同银行的账户间转账,可以是对个人的,也可以是对公司的。

2. check [tʃek] n. American spelling of cheque, a printed piece of paper that you write an amount of money on, sign, and use instead of money to pay for things 支票

    e.g. Can I pay by check?

    我可以用支票付款么?

    e.g. They send me a cheque for $200.

    他们寄给我一张200美元的支票。

5. Informing Customers of the Receipt of Payment

Dear Mr. Wilson,

We are delighted to inform you that we have received your payment for your order No. 123 and No. 345 which have been shipped last week.

Thank you for your cooperation and trust! We believe the shipment will turn out to your entire satisfaction!

We hope that we can expand our business to our mutual benefit in the near future!

Yours sincerely,

×××

 Notes

1. turn out to 变成；结果是

    e.g. Difficulties and obstacles, if properly understood and used, can turn out to be an unexpected source of strength.

    困难和障碍如果可以正确地了解和运用，可以出人意料地转变成力量的来源。

2. satisfaction [ˌsætisˈfækʃən] n. a feeling of happiness or pleasure because you have achieved something or got what you wanted 满足，满意

    to sb.'s satisfaction/to the satisfaction of sb. 使某人满意

    e.g. The order has executed to the entire satisfaction of customers.

    这笔订单执行令顾客完全满意。

    我们对你的样品满意的几种表达：

    Your sample satisfies us.

    We are satisfied with your sample.

    Your sample is found to our satisfaction.

    Your sample is found (to be) satisfactory.

3. expand [ikˈspænd] v. become or make larger or more extensive 扩大，扩展

    e.g. The computer industry has expanded greatly over the last decade.

    计算机行业在过去十年间大大地发展起来了。

4. mutual [ˈmjuːtʃʊəl] adj. (of a feeling or action) experienced or done by each or two or more parties towards the other or others (感情，行动) 相互的；彼此的

e.g. These two countries can work together for their mutual benefit and progress.
这两个国家可以为互惠和进步而合作。

6. Propose Acceptance of L/C Discrepancies

Dear Ms. Green,

Please find the discrepancies below mentioned by our bank.

L/C No. 345 stipulates the quantity of 5,000 units, but we only shipped 4,950 units for one 40' container. The rest 50 units will be delivered next time with PO#123.

The destination port was changed to Rotterdam, not Antwerp.

The above points have been already approved by your shipping colleagues. Please help to check and give Chartered Bank your acceptation and we could get the payment soon.

Thank you for your cooperation in advance.

Yours sincerely,

×××

Notes

1. discrepancy [dis'krepənsi] n. a difference between two amounts, details, reports etc. that should be the same（两个本该一样的数量、细节、报告等的）不一致、不符、差异；出入

   e.g. In case of quality discrepancy, claim should be lodged by the buyers within 30 days after the arrival of the goods at the port of destination.
   如果货物品质异议,买方应在货到目的口岸30天内提出索赔。

   e.g. We regret to find that there is a discrepancy in the amount of your L/C.
   我们很遗憾地发现你方信用证金额有误。

2. Chartered Bank (Standard Chartered Bank) 渣打银行
   一些主要的银行中英文对照如下：
   HSBC 汇丰银行
   Hang Seng Bank 恒生银行
   Citibank 花旗银行

Deutsche Bank 德意志银行

SBC 瑞士银行

ABN 荷兰银行

BOC(HK) 中国银行(香港)

7. Proposing New Payment Terms of Order

Dear Ms. Liu,

We are pleased that the business between us has proved to be very smooth and successful. Our past purchase of "Flying-pigeon" Brand bicycles from you has been paid as a rule by confirmed and irrevocable letter of credit.

On this basis, it has indeed cost us a great deal. From the moment we open the credit till the time our buyers pay us, our funds are tied up for about four months. Under the present circumstances, this question is particular taxing due to the tight money conditions and the unprecedentedly high bank interest. If you would kindly grant easier payment terms, we are sure that such an accommodation would be encouraging more business. We propose payment either by T/T or D/P at 60 days.

Your kindness in giving priority to the consideration of the above request and giving us an early favorable reply.

Yours faithfully,

×××

  Notes

1. easy ['i: zi] *adj.* （价格、报盘等）易于接受的；（市场、行情等）疲软的

    easy terms 易于接受的条件

    e.g. Please make your offer as easy as possible.

    请把你们的报价尽量容易接受。

    e.g. The market has turned easy.

    市场变得疲软。

2. as a rule 通常（= usually）

    e.g. I go to school by bus as a rule.

    我通常坐公车去学校。

3. tie up for about four months

   e.g. Our funds are tied up for about four months.

   我们的资金要被冻结约4个月。

   tie up 冻结资金，占用而积压资金

   e.g. It is expensive for us to open an L/C and it will tie up the capital of a small company like ours, so it is better for us to adopt the collection of D/P or D/A.

   开立信用证费用很高，会影响到像我方这样小公司的资金周转。因此最好采用付款交单或承兑交单的托收方式。

4. taxing ['tæksiŋ] adj. needing a lot of effort 难于负担的；使人感到压力的

   e.g. The job turned out to be more taxing than I'd expected.

   后来发觉这个工作比我原来想的要辛苦。

5. due to 由于【同义】owing to, because of, on account of

   e.g. The manager was late due to traffic jam.

   由于堵车经理迟到了。

   e.g. The conclusion of this business is due to the effort of staff.

   由于大家的努力，这笔交易达成了。

6. unprecedentedly [ʌn'presidentidli] adv. 空前地，前所未有地，史无前例地

   e.g. unprecedentedly high bank interest 前所未有的高额银行利息

   e.g. The investor enjoyed favorable development on an unprecedented scale.

   该投资人以空前的规模取得了有利进展。

7. accommodation [əˌkɒmə'deiʃn] n. 照顾；通融

   e.g. As a special accommodation, we will accept time L/C at 30 days.

   作为一种特殊的照顾，我们接受30天期限的信用证。

   e.g. We extend to you this accommodation in view of our friendly relations.

   考虑到我们俩的友谊，再次给予通融照顾。

   accommodate v. 照顾；通融

   e.g. We hope you will accommodate us by allowing 3% commission.

   希望你们可以照顾我们，给我们3%的佣金。

8. priority [prai'ɒrəti] n. the most important thing you have to do or deal with, or must be done or dealt with before everything else you have to do 优先处理的事

   give priority to something or someone, you treat them as more important than anything or anyone else 优先考虑

   e.g. Although you have a lot of transaction this year, we still hope you give priority to our order of such big quantity.

   虽然你们今年业务很多，我们仍然希望你们优先考虑我们这样一笔大订单。

   e.g. The exporter should give priority to the consideration of the goods' quality.

   出口商应该优先考虑商品的质量问题。

Part IV Useful Expressions and Sentences

Expressions

1. terms of payment 付款条件,付款方式
2. remittance 汇款,汇付
3. collection 托收
4. confirmed, irrevocable, documentary, transferrable, divisible Letter of Credit 保兑的、不可撤销的、跟单的、可转让的、可分割的信用证
5. T/T (Telegraphic Transfer) 电汇
6. M/T (Mail Transfer) 信汇
7. D/D (Demand Transfer) 票汇
8. D/P at sight; D/P after sight 即期付款交单;远期付款交单
9. D/A 承兑交单
10. under(on) ... terms 按……方式 on ... basis 在……基础上
11. D/P 30 days after the B/L date 提单日期后 30 天付款交单
    D/P 45 days after the draft date 汇票日期后 45 天付款交单
    D/A 90 days after sight 见票后 90 天承兑交单
12. telex release 提单电放
13. draw on sb. 向某人开汇票
14. as a special accommodation 作为特殊照顾
15. take/regard sth. as a precedent 把……作为先例
16. original documents 单据正本
17. balance 余款,尾款
18. easier payment terms 较宽松的支付方式
19. settle 付清(欠款)
20. tie up 冻结资金,占用而积压资金

Typical Sentences

1. Please send us the inspection report soon. We should submit all the documents for L/C negotiation.
2. In view of our long business relations, we will make an exception to our rules and accept L/C at 30 days.
3. We regret that we are unable to consider your request for payment on D/A terms.

4. In compliance with your request, we have made an exception to accept delivery against D/P at sight. However, this should not be taken as a precedent in future shipments.

5. We are glad to inform you that we have received your remittance.

6. Please help to settle the rest payment USD 5,000 to our bank account soon.

7. If you would kindly grant easier payment terms, we are sure that such an accommodation would be encouraging more business.

8. We would appreciate it if you can pay the total amount to us in advance by T/T not later than September 30th.

9. We have to request you to do business on the basis of confirmed, irrevocable L/C payable by draft at sight.

10. As it is our usual practice to require payment by sight L/C, we cannot see a precedent for this transaction.

Part Ⅴ Practical Training

Ⅰ. Elementary Training

1. Choose the best answer.

(1) For future transactions, D/A will only be accepted if the amount ____ is not up to EUR 2,000.
   A. involves   B. involved   C. involving   D. involve

(2) We will draw ____ you by our documentary draft at sight on collection basis.
   A. at   B. up   C. on   D. for

(3) Our company is prepared to accept a conditional price concession, provided the deal is to be paid partly ____ cash and partly ____ L/C.
   A. in, in   B. by, by   C. by, in   D. in, by

(4) Thank you for your remittance of USD 2,150.00 ____ the 80% freight due under Invoice No. 228.
   A. of paying   B. pay for   C. for payment   D. in payment of

(5) If you are unable to ____ your account by the end of next week, I am afraid we will be forced to take legal actions.
   A. decide   B. solve   C. pay   D. settle

(6) We trust that a letter of credit in our favor ____ the above-mentioned goods will

be established immediately.

　　A. including　　B. relating　　C. covering　　D. about

(7) The above mentioned are our usual terms of payment and also the payment methods commonly used in our foreign ____ in China.

　　A. practice　　B. habit　　C. custom　　D. rule

(8) It is our usual practice to require sight L/C. We cannot make an ____ with this transaction.

　　A. example　　B. exception　　C. experience　　D. excellence

(9) Documentary draft is a draft ____ by documents, such as bill of lading, invoice and insurance policy.

　　A. companied　　B. accorded　　C. companioned　　D. accompanied

(10) Having some difficulty in opening the L/C, our buyer eventually wanted to place an order ____ D/A basis.

　　A. for　　B. by　　C. on　　D. against

(11) Our payment terms are ____, irrevocable letter of credit for the invoice value.

　　A. confirmed　　B. combined　　C. committed　　D. completed

(12) As we must adhere ____ our customary practices, we hope that you will not think us unaccommodating.

　　A. with　　B. by　　C. at　　D. to

(13) Payment should be made ____ sight draft.

　　A. by　　B. on　　C. at　　D. after

(14) We have made ____ that we would accept D/P terms for your present order.

　　A. clear　　B. it is clear　　C. that　　D. it clear

(15) In view of the amount of this transaction ____ very small, we are prepared to accept payment by D/P at 60 days' sight for this order only.

　　A. is　　B. be　　C. being　　D. was

2. Read the following letters and fill in each blank with prepositions.

Letter 1

Dear Ms. Miller,

　　We refer __(1)__ your Contract Number 127 covering lumber __(2)__ the amount of $ 4,000 and Contract No. 766 __(3)__ iron pipes __(4)__ the amount of $ 6,000.

　　Since both contracts are less than 10,000 __(5)__ value, we would like you to accept D/P as the terms of payment.

We hope that this arrangement will meet with your approval and look forward to your early reply.

Yours sincerely,

× × ×

Letter 2

Dear Mr. Cooper,

We have received your letter in which you ask for easier terms __(1)__ payment.

In consideration of the very pleasant business relationship we have had with your firm for more than 10 years, we have decided to agree __(2)__ your suggestion. We shall, therefore, in future draw __(3)__ you __(4)__ 60 days, documents __(5)__ acceptance, and trust that this term will meet your requirements.

We hope that our concession will lead to a considerable increase of your orders. We can assure you that we will always try our best to execute them to your complete satisfaction.

Yours sincerely,

× × ×

3. **Translate the following English into Chinese.**

(1) easier payment terms

(2) a confirmed, irrevocable L/C

(3) as a special accommodation

(4) on D/A basis

(5) telex release

(6) tie up

(7) settle the balance

(8) original documents

(9) D/P 30 days after the draft date

(10) Telegraphic Transfer

(11) Your total check was US$ 900, and the enclosed check for US$ 58 is your refund.

(12) This transaction has been concluded on the basis of payment by letter of credit at sight.

(13) The only way to do this business is to effect payment by T/T at the time of loading.

(14) In view of our friendly relationship between us, we agree to accept 60 days' D/P.

(15) We are glad to inform you that we have received your remittance.

(16) Please keep us posted if you're experiencing the balance. Thank you!

(17) Our bank refused to accept these documents due to the discrepancy.

(18) All banking charges, including discrepancy fee and any wire commission will be deducted from the proceeds.

(19) Please make payment in Australian dollars into our ABN account.

(20) In compliance with your request, we have made an exception to accept delivery against D/P at sight. However, this should not be taken as a precedent in future shipments.

II. Intermediate Training

1. Supply the missing words in the blanks of the following letter. The first letters are given.

Dear Mr. Loake,

Thank you for your letter dated December 5th, reminding us that we did not settle our payment d____ on November 30th. A____ checking, we found that our accounting department made an oversight in settling the check to you.

Please find attached c____ for the amount of HK$ 5,000. We are sorry for the i____ caused and hope you will realize that we had no intention in d____ our payment.

Yours sincerely,

×××

2. Cloze. Choose the most suitable words from the list of words to fill in the blanks Each word can be used only once.

balance   customized   placing   confirmation   documents

Dear Sirs,

Thank you for ___(1)___ an order with us for 2,000 sets of 12V Power Tools. Our sales contract is attached to this letter. The products contain ___(2)___ design according to your specification. For this reason, in the sales contract we require a down payment.

The detailed clause of the payment terms in the S/C reads: The down payment up to 30% of the total contract amount shall be remitted to the seller no later than September 30th, 2019. The ___(3)___ shall be paid to the seller by T/T within 7 working days after receipt of the copy of shipping ___(4)___.

We expect your early ___(5)___.

Yours faithfully,

×××

Encl: A Sales Contract

 3. Translate the following Chinese into English.
(1) 我们希望你们能接受付款交单,信用证付款对我们来说不是很方便。
(2) 如果你们想在我们的市场扩大业务,就必须采取灵活的付款方式。
(3) 用信用证付款是我们对所有新客户的惯例。
(4) 在此推销阶段,我们将考虑接受付款交单方式以资鼓励。
(5) 我们财务部门在安排转账时打错了你们的公司名。

Ⅲ. Advanced Training

你是新艺纺织品公司的业务员,你之前刚和 Becker Glove 公司有过一笔业务,但 80,000 美元贷款已经到期 40 天。我方于一个月前已经去函催款的情况下,仍未收到回复。现在需要给 Becker Glove 公司再写一封催款函,要点如下:
(1) 至今未收到一月前写出的催款信的回复,表示遗憾。
(2) 希望解释迟付的原因,提出 5 天的还款期限。
(3) 回顾过去的合作,期望此类事情不再发生。

Module 7
Claims and Settlement
索赔及理赔

Unit 10 Complaints, Claims and Settlement
投诉,索赔及理赔

Lead-in

Try to finish the following tasks and find out the learning objectives of this unit.

Task 1

假设你需要撰写一封投诉信,抱怨货物与样品不一致。内容如下:

敬启者:

我们已于今日收到我方5月10日所订货物。经审查,发现不是所有货物都与贵方原先发来的样品相符,部分货物质量更差、重量更轻。因此现将该批货物退还贵方,运费到付。

Task 2

假设你需要撰写一封投诉信,抱怨交货延迟。内容如下:

敬启者:

作为很好的业务伙伴,我们已合作三年之久。在此期间,我们对于你方交货时效很满意。贵方的准时交货,给了我们充分的时间来满足活跃的市场需求。然而,最近贵方开始延迟交货,服务变得越来越不可靠。由于贵方的延误,我方已经无法赶在最后期限前交易,因此蒙受巨大损失。

Part Ⅰ Introduction

在进出口业务执行合同过程中,签约双方都应该严格履行合同义务。如一方未履行或未全部履行自己的义务,即构成违约。在这种情况下,受损的一方要求改善或补偿时,即为投诉(Complaint)。受损方有权根据合同规定向责任方提出损害赔偿的要求,即为索赔

(Claim)。责任方就受损方提出的要求进行处理,即为理赔(Settlement)。

导致申诉和索赔的原因大致有:

(1) 质量问题(Quality):货物的品质和规格与合同规定不符,质量低劣。

(2) 数量问题(Quantity):货物数量短缺。

(3) 交期问题(Time of Delivery):货物延误,未在预定时效期内到达。

(4) 其他问题(Other Cases):货物包装不良,或货物损毁等。

赔偿的内容可以有如下几个方面:

(1) 请求赔偿损失。

(2) 请求补运。货物短少和短交时,可请求补运。

(3) 请求调换。货物的品质不符或规格不符,可请求调换。

(4) 请求修理。产品发生故障或损坏时,可请求修理。

(5) 请求减价或折让。如交货延迟、品质不佳,皆可要求减价或贬值折让。

(6) 拒收货物,请求退还货物,并赔偿损失。

索赔程序:

(1) 索赔声明。发现问题后应在合同索赔期内通知对方,并声明保留索赔权利。

(2) 准备证明文件。索赔时务必提出证据,作为证明文件。

(3) 正式索赔。备齐证明文件,发出索赔函电。

索赔解决方法:

(1) 和解(Compromise)

(2) 调解(Mediate)

(3) 仲裁(Arbitration)

(4) 诉讼(Lawsuit)

Part Ⅱ Letter Writing Guide

As the purpose of complaining is to get better service, the more specific your letter is, the easier it will be for your correspondent to handle your complaint. Usually a claim or complaint letter follows the under-mentioned outline:

(1) The opening states the problem and gives as much information as possible. To state the problem suffered in detail.

(2) The body gives, if any, additional information—why it is necessary to write, why and how you are inconvenienced that is made by this error and so on.

(3) To present the evidence to support your complaints and claims.

(4) The body also states what you want to be done—what you consider a reasonable demand to satisfy your claim and settle the problem.

The following rules should be followed by the seller when dealing with a complaint:

(1) The first thing that has to be decided is whether the complaint is justified. If it is so, the sellers have to admit it readily, express his or her regret and agree to the buyer's request.

(2) If the complaint or claim is not justified, point this out politely and in agreeable manner. It would be a wrong policy to reject the customer's request.

(3) If the seller cannot deal with a complaint promptly, acknowledge it at once; explain that the matter is being investigated and a full reply will be sent later.

There is no need for sellers to go into a long story of how the mistake was made and a short explanation may be useful.

Part Ⅲ   Sample Letters

1. Making a Complaint on Poor Quality

Dear Sirs,

We have received the automatic coffee machines of the order No. 456 last week and we are sorry to tell you that the quality of it is very bad. Half of them could not work properly.

As so many products are of low quality, we require you refund the invoice amount and inspection fee of the goods amounting RMB 30,000,000. In support of our claim, we will send you a survey report issued by CIQ.

We hope you will settle this claim immediately. As soon as it is settled down, we will send the goods back to you. All the expenses will be for your account.

Sincerely yours,

ABC Co., Ltd.

 Notes

1. complaint [kəmˈpleint] n. 投诉,申诉;抱怨,不满
   表示不满的原因、抱怨的话时为可数名词,表示抽象的抱怨行为时为不可数名词。

e. g. Recently we received many complaints from our customers.

最近我们收到了很多客户的投诉。

complain v. 投诉

complaint about/ against/ that ...

e. g. Many customers complain about the products.

许多客户投诉该产品。

2. quality [ˈkwɒləti] n. 质量；品质；优质；高标准 adj. 优质的；高质量的

   e. g. Everyone can greatly improve the quality of life.

   每个人都可以大大改善生活质量。

3. refund [ˈriːfʌnd , riˈfʌnd] n. 退款；返还款；偿还金额 v. 退还；退（款）；偿付

   e. g. If there is a delay of 12 hours or more, you will receive a full refund of the price of your trip.

   如果耽搁达到或超过12小时，你会得到旅费全额退款。

   refund sth. （to sb.）/ refund sb. sth. 给某人退款

   e. g. We will refund your money to you in full if you are not entirely satisfied.

   如果你并不感到完全满意，我们会退还全部金额。

4. claim [kleim] n. 声明；宣称；断言；索赔 v. 宣称；声称；断言；要求（拥有）；索取

   作名词时，常与动词 make, lodge, file, raise, put in, bring up 等搭配，表示索赔的原因、金额，后接介词 for，表示索赔对象，后接 against 或 on。

   e. g. You can make a claim on your insurance policy.

   你可按保险单索赔。

   to claim a compensation of... from somebody for something 为某事向某人索赔若干金额

5. CIQ（Entry-Exit Inspection and Quarantine of People's Republic of China）中国出入境检验检疫

6. survey report 检验报告

7. be for one's account 由谁承担，由谁支付（＝ be at one's expense）

2. Making a Complaint on Time of Delivery

Dear Sirs,

When we placed our order for Children's Wear on October 20th, we did so on the understanding that delivery could be by November 25th. We are surprised that we have not yet received the goods or any news from you as to when you can expect delivery.

As the time of shipment is now considerably overdue, we should be obliged by you informing us by return of the reason for the delay.

This is the first time in many years that we have bad reason to complain and we expect that you will look into the matter at once.

We have no doubt that you will do your utmost to ensure that our consignment arrives soon.

Yours faithfully,

×××

 Notes

1. understanding [ˌʌndəˈstændɪŋ] *n*. 理解；领悟；了解；协议；谅解；体谅 *adj*. 善解人意的；富有同情心的；体谅人的

   e.g. We finally came to an understanding about what hours we would work.

   我们最终就工作时间问题取得了一致意见。

   on the understanding that 在……条件下，基于……

   e.g. I can help you on the understanding that you study hard.

   我可以帮你但条件是你要努力。

2. overdue [ˌəʊvəˈdjuː] *adj*. （到期）未付的；未做的；过期的；早该发生的；早应完成的

   e.g. We recognize your financial problems, but your account is overdue.

   我们知道你的财务问题，但你的帐户是过期的。

3. obliged [əˈblaɪdʒd] *adj*. 感激的；感谢的

   e.g. I'd be obliged if you would keep this to yourself.

   如果你保守这个秘密，我将感激不尽。

4. doubt [daʊt] *n*. 疑惑，疑问；不确定；不相信；*v*. 无把握；不能肯定；认为……未必可能；怀疑；不相信，不信任

   e.g. There is no doubt at all that we did the right thing.

   毫无疑问我们做得对。

   e.g. No one doubted his ability.

   没有人怀疑他的能力。

5. consignment [kənˈsaɪnmənt] *n*. 装运的货物；运送物；发送；投递，递送

   e.g. The first consignment of food has already left for Italy.

   运送的第一批食品已经发往意大利。

3. Making a Complaint on Service

Gentlemen:

Our Order No. 1510

We duly received the documents and took delivery of the goods on arrival of M. V. "Pearl" at Hamburg.

We are much obliged to you for the prompt execution of this order. Everything appears to be correct and in good condition expect Case No. 11.

Unfortunately when we opened this case we found it contained completely different articles, and we can only presume a mistake was made and then contents of the case were for another order.

I'm disappointed with your service. As we need the articles we ordered to complete deliveries to our new customers, we must ask you to arrange for the dispatch of replacements at once. We attach a list of the contents of case No. 11, and shall be glad if you will check this with our order and the copy of your invoice.

In the meantime we are holding the above mentioned case at your disposal. Please let us know what you wish us to do with it.

×××

 Notes

1. execution [ˌeksɪˈkjuːʃn] n. 处决;实行;执行;实施;表演;(乐曲的)演奏

    e.g. Her idea was good, but her execution of the scheme was disastrous.
    她的构想很好,但实行起来却糟糕透顶。

2. presume [prɪˈzjuːm] v. 假设,假定;推定;设定;设想

    e.g. We mustn't presume too much upon the reliability of such sources.
    我们不应过分指望这类消息来源的可靠性。

3. dispatch [dɪˈspætʃ] n. 派遣,调遣;发送;急件,快信 v. 派遣,调遣;派出;发送;迅速处理,迅速办妥,迅速完成

    e.g. Goods are dispatched within 24 hours of your order reaching us.

订单到达我方 24 小时内发货。

4. replacement [ri'pleismənt] n. 调换;替代关系;取替,替代,替换

e.g. If the warranty is limited, the terms may entitle you to a replacement or refund.
如果保修有限制,根据条款你也许可以要求退换或者退款。

5. disposal [di'spəʊzl] n. 去掉;清除;处理;(企业、财产等的)变卖,让与

e.g. They're practices that include every aspect of business-invention, definition, construction, production and the ultimate disposal of the product.
它们都是技能,涉及商业的每一个方面,发明、定义、施工、生产和最终产品的处置。

4. Lodging a Claim on Damage of the Goods

Dear Sir,

Re: Claim on TV Sets

The captioned goods you shipped per M.V. "Victoria" on May 15th arrived here yesterday.

On examination, we have found that many of the TV sets are severely damaged, though the cases themselves show no trace of damage.

Considering this damage was due to the rough handling by the steamship company, we claimed on them for recovery of the loss, but an investigation made by the surveyor has revealed the fact that the damage is attributable to improper packing. For further particulars, we refer you to the surveyor's report enclosed.

We are, therefore, compelled to claim on you to compensate us for the loss of $ 27,900, which we have sustained by the damage to the goods.

We trust that you will be kind enough to accept this claim and deduct the sum claimed from the amount of your next invoice to us.

Yours truly,

×××

 Notes

1. lodge [lɒdʒ] n. 乡间小屋,小舍;门房;管理员室;传达室 v. 正式提出;租住

e.g. This country has lodged a complaint with the International Court of Justice.

该国已向国际法院提出了申诉。

2. rough [rʌf] *adj*. 粗糙的；不平滑的；高低不平的；不确切的；粗略的；大致的；粗暴的，粗野的；猛烈的

e.g. This watch is not designed for rough treatment.

这块手表不可重拿重放。

3. recovery [riˈkʌvəri] *n*. 恢复；痊愈；改善；回升；复苏；取回；收回；复得

e.g. There is a reward for information leading to the recovery of the missing diamonds.

凡能为找回丢失的钻石提供线索者可获奖赏。

4. reveal [riˈviːl] *v*. 揭示；显示；透露；显出；露出；展示

e.g. He cannot reveal how much money is involved in the scheme.

他不能透露该计划投入了多少钱。

5. attributable [əˈtribjətəbl] *adj*. 可归因于；可能由于

attributable to sb. / sth. 归因于某人／某事

e.g. Their illnesses are attributable to a poor diet.

他们的病可能是不良饮食所致。

6. particular [pəˈtikjuləz] *n*. 细节；详情 *adj*. 专指的，特指的；不寻常的；格外的；特别的

e.g. The new contract will be the same in every particular as the old one.

新合同与旧合同的各项细节将完全相同。

7. compel [kəmˈpel] *v*. 强迫，迫使；(使)必须；引起(反应)

e.g. Bad weather compelled them to stay at home.

恶劣的天气迫使他们呆在家里。

8. sustain [səˈstein] *v*. 维持(生命、生存)；(使)保持；(使)稳定持续；遭受，蒙受；经受

e.g. The company sustained losses of millions of dollars.

公司遭受了数百万美元的巨大损失。

9. deduct [diˈdʌkt] *v*. (从总量中)扣除，减去

e.g. The company deducted this payment from his compensation.

公司从他获得的赔偿金中扣去了这笔付款。

5. Making a Complaint on Inferior Packing

Dear Sirs,

We refer to Sales Contract No. 324 covering the purchase of 5,000 metric tons of white crystal sugar.

The consignment arrived on April 30th. On inspection, we found that 200 bags had burst and that the contents, estimating at 8,000 kg, had been irretrievably lost. We proceeded to have a survey report made. The report has now confirmed our initial findings. The report indicates that the loss was due to the use of substandard bags for you, which are responsible.

On the strength of the survey report, we hereby register our claim against you as follows:

Short delivered quantity US$ 180

Survey charges US$ 60

Total claimed US$ 240

We enclose our survey report No. SR247 and look forward to early settlement of the claim.

×××

 Notes

1. burst [bɜːst] v. (使)爆裂,胀开;猛冲;突然出现;爆满 n. 突发;迸发;爆破;爆裂

    e.g. That balloon will burst if you blow it up any more.

    你再给气球充气,它就要爆了

2. irretrievably [ˌɪrɪˈtriːvəbli] adv. 不能挽回地;不能补救地

    e.g. Some of our old traditions are irretrievably lost.

    我们的一些老传统已经失传。

3. substandard [ˌsʌbˈstændəd] adj. 不达标的;不合格的

    e.g. We object to dumping substandard machines on the market.

    我们反对将次品机器向市场倾销。

4. register [ˈredʒɪstə(r)] v. 登记;注册;提出主张;记录

    e.g. China has registered a protest over foreign intervention.

    中国对外国干涉正式提出了抗议。

6. Lodging a Claim on Weight Shortage

Dear Sirs,

Referring to our letter of March 17th, 2020, in connection with the rice under the contract No. AB683 shipped Per S.S. "Blue Bird". After discharged at Dalian, we found that there is a short-weight of 1,357 M/T and therefore we are now filing a claim with

you as follows:

Claim Number	Claim for	
DL01	Short-weight	US$ 1,368.60
DL02	Quality	US$ 1,532.31
	Total Amount	US$ 2,900.91

In order to support our claim, we are sending you herewith one copy of Inspection Certificates No. DCIB011 and DCIB012 respectively together with our Statement of the Claim which amounts to US$ 2,900.91.

Please give our claim your most favorable consideration and let us have your settlement at an early date.

Yours faithfully,

×××

 Notes

1. discharge [dis'tʃɑ:dʒ, 'distʃɑ:dʒ] v. 准许(某人)离开;解雇;释放;流出 n. 排出(物);流出(物);获准离开;免职;出院;退伍;(任务或职责的)履行,执行;(债务的)清偿

    e.g. Patients were being discharged from the hospital too early.

    病人都过早获准出院。

2. herewith [ˌhiə'wið] adv. 随同此信(或书、文件)

    e.g. I enclose herewith a copy of the policy.

    我随信附上一份保险单。

3. favorable ['feivərəbl] adj. 赞许的;赞同的;有利的;顺利的;令人愉快的

    e.g. Compared with the market prices of other countries, ours is still favorable.

    和其他国家的市场价相比,这已经很优惠了。

7. Writing a Letter Settling the Claim

Dear Sirs,

Thank you for your letter of May 16th in which you lodged a claim for short delivery of 8,000 kg of white cement.

We wish to express our deep regret for this incident. We have checked our warehouse and discovered that part of consignment was not packed as specified in the contract. This was due to the negligence of our warehouse staff. We therefore enclose a cheque for US＄ 1,240 in full and final settlement of your claim.

We trust that this unfortunate error will not adversely affect our future relations.

× × ×

Notes

1. incident ['insidənt] n. 发生的事情(尤指不寻常的或讨厌的)；严重事件，冲突

    e.g. These incidents were the latest in a series of disputes between the two nations.
    这些事件是两国一系列争端中最近发生的几起。

2. specify ['spesifai] v. 具体说明；明确规定；详述；详列

    e.g. The contract clearly specifies who can operate the machinery.
    合同明确规定谁可以操作机器。

3. negligence ['neglidʒəns] n. 疏忽；失职；失误；过失

    e.g. The accident was caused by negligence on the part of the driver.
    事故是由于司机的过失造成的。

4. adversely ['ædvɜːsli] adv. 反而；不利地；逆地；反对地

    e.g. Price changes must not adversely affect the living standards of the people.
    物价变化一定不能给人们的生活水准带来负面影响。

Part Ⅳ Useful Expressions and Sentences

Expressions

1. complain about/against ... 抱怨，投诉……
2. raise/lodge a claim 提出索赔
3. accept a claim 同意索赔
4. reject a claim 拒绝索赔
5. settle a claim 解决索赔，理赔
6. be for one's account 由谁承担，由谁支付(＝be at one's expense)
7. on the understanding that 在……条件下，基于……
8. look into 考察；调查；研究
9. no doubt that 毫无疑问的是
10. take delivery 提货

11. in good condition 状态良好
12. complete delivery 交付,付清
13. at one's disposal 任某人处理;供某人任意使用;由某人自行支配
14. rough handling 粗鲁搬运
15. on the strength of 在……的影响下;凭借;依赖
16. in full 所有地;全部地;全数地

Typical Sentences

1. We are sorry to complain to you about the delay in shipment which has caused us much trouble.
2. Upon examination, we discovered to our surprise that they were inferior in quality.
3. Although the quality of these goods is not up to the sample, we are prepared to accept them if you reduce the price by 5%.
4. We are sorry to learn that the quality of your shipment is not up to the agreed specifications.
5. We think that the damage was caused by improper packing.
6. We reserved the right to claim compensation from you for any damage.
7. We filed a claim against you for the short weight.
8. Your shipment of our Order No. 46 has been found short weight by 1,000 kilos.
9. We have to lodge a claim against you on this shipment for US$ 2,880 on account of short weight.
10. We have received your remittance in settlement of our claim.

Part Ⅴ　Practical Training

Ⅰ. Elementary Training

1. Choose the best answer.

(1) We regret to have to complain ____ the bad quality of shipment of sugar by S. S. "Taishan".

  A. at   B. about   C. on   D. in

(2) The goods under Contract No. 123 left here ____.

  A. in a good condition   B. in good conditions

C. in good condition   D. in the good condition

(3) We have lodged a claim ____ ABC Co. ____ the quality of the goods shipped ____ S.S. "Peace".
   A. against, on, by   B. with, for, under
   C. on, against, as per   D. to, for, per

(4) As the goods are ready for shipment, we ____ your L/C to be opened immediately.
   A. hope   B. anticipate   C. await   D. expect

(5) Our customers have claimed ____ us ____ delayed delivery of the goods.
   A. on, for   B. with, about   C. against, for   D. from, in

(6) They claimed compensation ____ the value ____ the missing package ____ the carrier.
   A. for, for, for   B. for, on, for
   C. for, of, from   D. with, of, with

(7) We reserve the right to claim ____ the cargoes shipped ____ us.
   A. on, on   B. on, for   C. on, to   D. for, for

(8) The buyers shall lodge any claim for this consignment ____ the sellers ____ 30 days ____ arrival of the goods, after which time none will be entertained.
   A. on, for, on   B. on, for, upon
   C. against, for, after   D. against, within, after

(9) We have placed your claim ____ inferior quality ____ the manufactures ____ their consideration.
   A. on, for, for   B. for, for, after
   C. on, before, for   D. for, to, after

(10) In such circumstances, we cannot but lodge our claim ____ the Arbitration Committee ____ you for the value of the goods damaged.
   A. before, against   B. with, for   C. with, with   D. for, against

(11) Our customers insist that they ____ this claim against you for damage.
   A. be justified in filing   B. justify to file
   C. are justified to file   D. are justified at filing

(12) The goods ____ to be damaged by sea water if stowed on deck.
   A. liable   B. in liable   C. incline   D. are liable

(13) The goods are to be packed ____ wooden cases, wrapped ____ matting outside.
   A. with, with   B. with, in   C. in, with   D. in, in

(14) We suggest that this material ____ packed ____ tins of 625 grams, 48 tins ____ one wooden case.

A. is, with, in   B. is, in, in   C. be, with, in   D. be, in, to

2. Read the following letters and fill in each blank with prepositions.

Letter 1

Dear Sirs,

　　We have received your letter __(1)__ June 15th, informing us that the sewing machines we shipped to you arrived __(2)__ a damaged condition __(3)__ account of imperfectness of our packing.

　　__(4)__ receipt of your letter, we have given this matter our immediate attention. We have studied your surveyor's report very carefully.

　　We are convinced that the present damage was due to extraordinary circumstances under which they were transported to you. We are therefore not responsible __(5)__ the damage; but as we do not think that it would be fair to have you bear the loss alone, we suggest that loss be divided between both of us, to which we hope you will agree.

Yours sincerely,

×××

Letter 2

Dear Sirs,

　　I refer to your letter of October 25th regarding the ABC Company's delivery service. I appreciate it highly for bringing this __(1)__ my attention. I feel so sorry that the delays __(2)__ delivery are very damaging.

　　Having checked with our forwarding agent, it is clear that you have to wait a long time for recent shipping arrangement, and we, too, find this unacceptable. I really must apologize __(3)__ the inconvenience you have been caused. I can assure you that we are currently considering switch transport company to avoid this type of error occurring again.

　　We take all our customers' comments seriously. With this __(4)__ mind, we are more than happy to make special arrangements to have your order No. 1234 delivered in the next 2 days.

Please accept my apologies once again ___(5)___ the inconvenience.

× × ×

3. Translate the following English into Chinese.

(1) raise/lodge a claim

(2) rough handling

(3) settle a claim

(4) complain about/against ...

(5) accept a claim

(6) in good condition

(7) for one's account

(8) at one's disposal

(9) We hope you will inform us of the reason for delay.

(10) We are not in a position to entertain your claim.

(11) We discovered that they were altogether inferior in quality to the sample.

(12) It is preferable if you can dispose of them in your market.

(13) Please examine the matter and send us the replacement of the 4 missing boxes.

(14) We reserve the right to claim compensation from you for the damage.

(15) This is the maximum concession we can afford.

II. Intermediate Training

1. Supply the missing words in the blanks of the following letter. The first letters are given.

Dear Sirs,

100 Bales Pure Wool by S. S. "Victoria"

The c____ goods have been inspected carefully upon a____ in Hamburg and we enclose the Weight Note i____ by the swore inspectors.

You will see from the Weight Note that there is a s____ of 41 kg, or about 91 lb in the shipment.

We have noticed lately that several of your s____ have turned o____ to short weight, though this was formerly never the case. Such losses are cutting d____ our small p____ and we think any such shortage will not be a____ to happen again.

We look forward to receiving your suggestion on how you i____ to reimburse us for this short weight.

Looking forward to your early reply.

Yours faithfully,

×××

2. Cloze. Choose the most suitable words from the list of words to fill in the blanks. Each word can be used only once.

penalty　　standard　　negligence　　quantity　　discrepancy
inferior　　wrong goods　　packing　　complaints　　delay

Complaints are often received by companies who ship consignments overseas. Since complaints are about the __(1)__ delivered, perhaps not enough goods were sent, perhaps too many. And it is always a cause for complaint that the __(2)__ are delivered. Often there are complaints about poor __(3)__, which can cause damage to the goods. Sometimes the complaints are about __(4)__ quality. In this case, buyers often complain that the goods are not up to the __(5)__. There may be a __(6)__ between the samples and the goods which actually arrive.

A complaint may be about a __(7)__ in shipment. Usually, there is a __(8)__ clause in the contract to protect the buyer against loss from delay.

__(9)__ about damage are usually the business of insurance companies, but if the damage is caused by the __(10)__ of the packer, then the insurance companies will not take responsibility.

3. Translate the following Chinese into English.

(1) 取消订单

(2) 装运延误

(3) 劣质

(4) 归因于

(5) 不足

(6) 保留权利

(7) 有毛病的

(8) 包装不慎

(9) 忽略,疏漏

(10) 我们的用户坚持你方应设法补偿他们所受到的损失。

(11) 我方接受贵公司对包装不良的正当投诉,并请贵公司将受损货物退还。

(12) 我方是以FOB价成交的,看来我方不应对短重负责。

(13) 因你方对我方的提议不满意,我方建议将此事提交仲裁。

(14) 发错货物是由于我方包装人员的错误造成的。

(15) 检验报告表明实际送达货物的重量与发票重量相差35公吨。

(16) 如果那箱丢失的货找不到,我们将保留对你方提出短量索赔的权利。

(17) 请立即办理此事并务必保证立即交货。

(18) 因有关货物质量低劣所造成的的损失,我们不得不要求你方赔偿。

(19) 出现任何损坏,我们保留向你方索赔的权利。

(20) 相信这是对你方最有利的解决办法,因为你方能以特殊价格购得所有货物。

Ⅲ. Advanced Training

 1. Translate the following letter into English.

敬启者:

感谢您寄来本公司于10月19日订购的北京服装。请您注意下列各点:

(1) 布料颜色与原样不同。

(2) 所附的绿色腰带与服装不配。

我方已另邮寄其中两件服装,并希望您全部更换为正确颜色的货品。有关运费一事,我方同意加付多出来的空运费用。同时,因为空运的包装及保险费较低,故请您考虑负担空运费用的一部分。

请及时告知贵公司对此事的处理意见。

 2. Write a letter in English.

Write a letter to complain of the delay in shipment stating the following facts:

(1) 所订货物收到,核对无误,情况良好。

(2) 本应8月底前到达的货物9月14日才到,致使我方交货压力甚大。

(3) 延误现象一再发生会致使客户转向他处,要求今后一定如期交货。

Module 8
Other Routine Works
其他日常工作

Unit 11　Other Routine Letters
其他日常工作的函电写作

Part Ⅰ　Introduction

在维持亲密的交易关系时,也应该注重其他的工作关系,比如日常出差的自动回复和一些商务通知:职务调动、休假、展会安排、公司新规定等等。这些函电写作虽不像交易类的函电写作一样正式,但是也有一定的写作原则。本单元将介绍常用的其他日常工作的函电。

Part Ⅱ　Letter Writing Guide

1. Automatic reply when you are on business 出差的自动回复

(1) Stating when you are on a business trip.

(2) Sending your temporary contact information.

(3) Showing sorry for the inconvenience.

2. Notice when you change your position 职务调动通知

(1) Informing that you have changed your position clearly.

(2) Clearly telling the customer who is responsible for following up on what is on hand and who can be contacted for the following process.

(3) Showing appreciating of the customer's understanding.

3. Notice when you have a holiday 休假的通知

(1) Specifying a specific date for the holiday.

(2) Making arrangements for existing orders and follow-up projects.

(3) Expressing hopes that the customer will understand.

4. Notice informing clients of exhibition arrangements 通知客户展会安排

(1) Informing existing and potential customers of specific exhibitions.

(2) Showing exhibition details.

(3) Expressing hope that clients will come to the exhibition.

5. Notice informing clients of new regulations 通知客户公司新规定

(1) Informing clients that your company has new regulations.

(2) Explaining the detailed information of new regulations.

(3) Expressing the hope that business will continue to grow.

Part Ⅲ   Sample Letters

1. Automatic Reply When You Are on Business

出差期间,往往不能在第一时间处理邮件,如果身在国外,甚至有可能两三天才会看一下邮箱。为了避免客户久等,或者错过某些重要事项,需要在邮箱里设置好自动回复,让客户知道有紧急的事情如何联系到你,或者应该联系谁。

Dear Sir or Madam,

I'm not in the office from July 15th to August 1st, and have limited time to check and reply emails in that period.

For any urgent business, please contact my colleague Ms. Jenny Chow at 852-***-***, and Jennychow@***.com.

Sorry for the inconvenience!

Best regards,

Cindy Liu

 Notes

1. 专业的业务员在出差或者休假前,可把自动回复的邮件写好两份,保存起来。一份是internal(内部的),另一份是external(外部的)。前者发给公司的同事,后者发给公司以外的人。邮件的侧重点可以有所不同。前者可以告诉同事,自己什么时候什么原因不在公司,有重要问题可以联系谁,有其他问题可以联系谁。而外部邮件通常都比较正式,只涉及业务方面的问题,应固定几个联系人负责公司的对外联系,这样就不会使客户感觉混乱。

2. contact ['kɒntækt] n. close interaction 接触,联系   vi./vt. be in or establish communication with (使)接触;联系

make contact with sb. 与某人联系

e.g. I finally made contact with her in Paris.

我最终在巴黎与她取得了联系。

e.g. Please contact me directly as Jack is on annual leave these days.

因为杰克最近在休年假,(有事)请直接与我联系。

e.g. I will contact him by telephone. 我会与他电话联系。

3. have limited time to do sth. 不太有时间做某事

e.g. I have limited time to check emails in the following days.

接下来几天我不太有时间查收邮件。

4. urgent ['ɜːdʒənt] adj. compelling immediate action 紧急的,急迫的

e.g. Please call my mobile for any top urgent business.

遇到任何非常紧急的事件,麻烦您直接打我手机。

2. Notice When You Change Your Position

职场上,必然会碰到工作上的调动,可能是内部的职位调动,也可能是去新的公司,这时候就需要在离开之前做好交接,明确告诉客户,手头上的工作由谁负责跟进,后面的流程可以联系谁。

Dear Bill,

Glad to inform you that I was promoted to the team leader for our purchasing department. Ms. Fanny Wang, my assistant in the past years, will hand over my work, and continue doing business with you!

Really need your help to contact with her for any issues from now on. I'm sure that she will pay more attention to your orders.

Thank you very much for your continued support in the past years! I will never forget everything you have done for me.

Best wishes,

William Lee

 Notes

1. promote [prə'məʊt] vt. give a promotion to or assign to a higher position 升职,晋升

e.g. I was promoted to editor and then editorial director.

我晋升为编辑,之后又晋升为编辑部主任。

2. hand over:give sb. the responsibility for dealing with a particular situation or problem 把某事交给某人负责,接管

   e.g. Mr. Zhang, my previous assistant in sales department, will hand over my job.

   我原先的助理,业务部的张先生将会接手我的工作。

3. continue [kənˈtinjuː] vi./vt. continue a certain state, condition, or activity 继续,延续

   e.g. Diana and Roy Jarvis are determined to continue working when they reach retirement age.

   戴安娜·贾维斯和罗伊·贾维斯决心到退休年龄后还继续工作。

   continued [kənˈtinjuːd] adj. without stop or interruption 继续的;持久的

3. Notice When You Have a Holiday

休假有两种情况,一种是个人的休假,比如年假、病假、婚假等;另一种是法定假期,或者整个公司的休假。遇到休假,要事先通知客户,并对现有的订单或跟进的项目作出交代,什么时候跟进,如何跟进,由谁负责跟进,都需要事先做好安排。

Dear Anna,

I will be on Annual Leave from July 10th to 25th, and will not check email during that period.

My assistant John will help me to reply emails then. Please contact him directly for any issues.

For very important or urgent problems, please do not hesitate to call my mobile.

Best regards,

Mike

 Notes

1. Annual Leave:paid time off work granted by employers to employees to be used for whatever the employee wishes 年假

   e.g. I'm on Annual Leave, and will be back to office next Monday.

   我正在休年假,下周一会回到公司。

   Sick Leave n. 病假   Home Leave 探亲假

2. be on holiday 在休假

 e.g. I will be on holiday from next Monday to Friday.

 我下周一到周五休假。

 e.g. Please note that Lily is on Sick Leave these days. You could write me emails directly.

 请注意 Lily 最近在休病假,(有关任何问题)您可以给我写邮件。

 e.g. Her company allows a 10-day Home Leave every year.

 她单位每年允许 10 天探亲假。

Dear Sir or Madam,

I will be out of office for Chinese New Year holiday from February 16th to 26th.

With very limited access to email, I'm afraid I can't check or reply your email in time.

If you have urgent matter to talk with me, please call me at +86-139 * * * * * * * *.

Thanks for your understanding and have a nice day!

                Yours faithfully,

                    Serena

 Notes

1. access ['ækses] n. a way of entering or leaving, the act of approaching or entering 进入,机会,常与 to 连用。

 e.g. The facilities have been adapted to give access to wheelchair users.

 这些设施已经过改装,使轮椅使用者能够进入。

 e.g. He was not allowed access to a lawyer.

 他未被允许接触律师。

2. with very limited access to 访问权限非常有限

4. Notice Informing Clients of Exhibition Arrangements

  如果决定参加某个展会,应在第一时间通知所有现在和潜在的客户,争取见面的机会。尤其是一些大型的综合性展会和国际行业展会,都有可能碰到现有客户或潜在客户,寻找合作机会。一般需要提前半个月通知,然后在展会三天前再通知一次,以免客户遗忘。

Dear Lisa,

Glad to inform you that we will attend the Canton Fair Phase Ⅱ & Phase Ⅲ this autumn.

Please find our booth number below:
Phase Ⅱ: 11.2A20-21
Phase Ⅲ: 10.1A12

Please visit our booth for reviewing our new seasonal products for 2019. Hope to meet you and Alex then.

Best wishes,

Lily Wang

Notes

1. attend [əˈtend] *vi./vt.* be present at (meetings, church services, university), etc. 出席
   e.g. Thousands of people attended the funeral.
   数千人参加了葬礼。
   e.g. The meeting will be attended by finance ministers from many countries.
   这次会议将有许多国家的财政部长出席。
2. phase [feiz] *n.* any distinct time period in a sequence of events 阶段;时期
   e.g. This autumn, 6,000 residents will participate in the first phase of the project.
   今年秋季,6,000 名居民将参与这项计划的第一阶段。
3. booth [buːð; buːθ] *n.* a small shop at a fair; for selling goods or entertainment 货摊
   e.g. Welcome to our booth. Which items are you interested in?
   欢迎来到我们的展位。您对哪些产品感兴趣?
4. seasonal [ˈsiːz(ə)n(ə)l] *adj.* occurring at or dependent on a particular season 季节的;周期性的
   e.g. The figures aren't adjusted for seasonal variations.
   这些数字未作季节性变化调整。

Dear Sir,

Jingxinli Digital Science & Technology Company Ltd. is pleased to invite you to attend The Sixth Chinese Commodities Fair, Sharjah on November 18th—22nd, 2017 in the International Trade Center Sharjah, UAE. Our Booth is No. 2A041.

Our company established in 1996. We take the sample machines with us for the Exhibition. Especially, with the new style Button making machine and Jigsaw Puzzle machine (Manual).

We appreciate that you will visit our Booth during the Exhibition.

If you have any questions or concerns, or if I may be of assistance in any way, please do not hesitate to contact me.

Wish to meet you soon in Sharjah.

Sincerely,

Jasmine
Sale Manager

 Notes

1. Sharjah [ˈʃɑːdʒə] n. 沙迦,是阿联酋的第三大酋长国
2. UAE(United Arab Emirates) 阿拉伯联合酋长国
3. Button making machine 按钮制造机
4. Jigsaw Puzzle machine 拼图机
5. manual [ˈmænjʊ(ə)l] adj. of or relating to the hands 手动的,手控的
    e.g. There is a manual pump to get rid of the water. 有一台手动水泵用来排水。
6. concern [kənˈsɜːn] n. something that interests you because it is important or affects you
    担心;担心的事,关心的事
    e.g. His concern was that people would know that he was responsible.
    他担忧的是人们会知道他应该负责任。
7. be of assistance 有帮助;有好处
    e.g. I will be of assistance where I can, my friend.
    我会尽一切可能协助你,我的朋友。

5. Notice Informing Clients of New Regulations

很多时候,公司会根据业务的发展,修改以往的合作模式或提出新的要求等。碰到这种情况,不能简单地通知客户,还需要出具一封正式的函电。如果是重要问题,不能放在邮件

的正文里，而要使用打印签字后的扫描件，通过邮件附件形式，正式告知客户。

Dear Marine,

I hereby announce that Miss Jacky Wang has left our company since May 31st, 2020.

Please contact with Ms. Jenny Chow from now on for any orders and projects which Jacky handled in the past time.

As per my discussion with our top management, they had interested to expand the business with your company, and could give you a better payment. T/T 45 days or D/P 45 days is acceptable for us. Please help to advise which one would you like.

I sincerely hope to keep and expand our current business this year.

Best regards,

Rachel Lin

 Notes

1. hereby [hiə'bai] adv. 以此方式
2. announce [ə'naʊns] v. make known; make an announcement 宣布
   e.g. He will announce tonight that he is resigning from office.
   他今晚将宣布他要辞职。
3. as per 按照；根据
   e.g. I approached an official, as per instructions.
   我按照指示接洽了一位官员。
4. expand business with sb. 与某人扩大贸易

Part Ⅳ Useful Expressions and Sentences

Expressions

1. make contact with sb. 与某人联系
2. have limited time to do sth. 做某事时间有限
3. hand over 移交给某人
4. Annual Leave 年假

5. Sick Leave 病假

6. Home Leave 探亲假

7. be on holiday 在度假

8. as per 按照，根据

9. be of assistance 有帮助

10. expand business with sb. 与某人扩大贸易

11. with very limited access to 访问权限非常有限

Typical Sentences

1. I have to reschedule my next trip to Osaka.
2. We will attend Canton Fair next month，with booth No. 198.
3. We are not sure if we will visit the London Fair this year.
4. Please contact colleague Michelle at michelle@hotmail.com.au.
5. I will be on Sick Leave for body check next Monday.
6. I will join in our human resource department next week due to the internal transfer.
7. We are committed to improving our communication channel for our future orders.
8. With very limited access to email, I'm afraid I can't check or reply your email in time.
9. If you have any questions or concerns, or if I may be of assistance in any way, please do not hesitate to contact me.
10. I hereby announce that Mrs. Wang has left our company since August 15th，2020.

Part Ⅴ   Practical Training

 1. Translate the following into English or Chinese.

(1) Have you visited the fairs in Dubai?

(2) You will find our new products display then.

(3) Please contact me directly because Jane is on Sick Leave these days.

(4) I couldn't check the emails every day because of my Sick Leave.

(5) I will not be in the office this afternoon due to the awful feeling.

(6) Our new factory will be commencing production in August and we would like to invite you and your wife to be present at a celebration party on August 1st.

(7) 很抱歉通知您，由于内部调动，我将不再负责贵公司的订单。

(8) 感谢您一直以来的鼓励和支持。

(9) 我下周二到周四休假。

(10) 我正在休年假，下周五会回到公司。

 2. Write an Annual Leave Announcement with the following information.

(1) 我将从下个月 10 号到 20 号休年假，在此期间不会查看邮箱。

(2) 我的助理 Alina 会帮我回复邮件，有事请直接联系她。

(3) 如果遇到紧急情况，请直接打我手机。

 3. Translate the following invitation letter into Chinese.

Dear Sir or Madam,

    We sincerely invite you to participate the Hong Kong Toys & Games Fair 2019 which is the largest toys fair in Asia and second in the world. The Fair, organized by Hong Kong Trade Development Council, sponsored by Federation of Hong Kong Industries, Hong Kong Toys Council and Toys Manufactures Association, will be held in Hong Kong Convention and Exhibition Center on and from January 8th to 11th, 2019.

    It is estimated that there will be more than 3,000 manufactures from over 50 countries and areas participating the fair. In the fair the exhibitors can not only exhibit their new products but also, through the series of seminars held in the fair, understand the latest development trends. The seminars will provide the circles with chances of exchanging information and sharing creative ideas and experiences.

    Hong Kong is the second biggest export area of toys in the world. The merchants here enjoy great prestige in the world. With all kinds of toys and other related products as well as a great variety of popular games in the exhibition, we are sure that the fair will satisfy both exhibitors and buyers. By its huge scale, rich and varied seminars, as well as extensive products choice, the fair will surely provide merchants in this circle with boundless business chances.

    Warmly welcome you to the fair.

                                                Sincerely yours,

                                                            × × ×

Unit 12　Holiday Greetings
节日问候

Lead-in

Try to finish the following tasks and find out the learning objectives of this unit.

Task 1

假设你是中国光明国际贸易有限公司（Guangming International Trading Co. Ltd.；Address：30 Sichuan Road，Shanghai，China；Tel：86-21-12345678；Fax：86-21-23456789；Email：guangming@hotmail.com）进出口部的经理。你公司曾与英国伦敦亚瑟父子公司（Messrs. Arthur Grey & Son Co.，Ltd.；Address：19 Cheapside，London，E. C. 2；Tel：0044-20-876543；Fax：0044-20-765432；Email：mags_ld@yahoo.com）合作，出口 100 台真空吸尘器（vacuum cleaner）。现在，圣诞节将至，请致函该公司，给予节日祝福。

注意信中务必包含以下内容：
(1) 圣诞节将至，我方预祝贵方度过一个快乐、兴旺的新年。
(2) 希望未来一年充满温暖、平和、幸福。
(3) 我方一直给予贵方诚挚、优惠的服务，希望未来一年也是一个快乐丰收年。一旦贵方对于产品有任何需求，请速与我方联系，我方将竭诚服务，不胜感激。

Task 2

假设你是中国上海的鸿利实业有限公司（HongLi Industrial Company；Address：123 Yishan Road，Xuhui District，Shanghai，China；Tel：86-21-87035689；Fax：86-21-87035688；Email：hlic@163.com）的经理 Louis 女士，最近与美国路易斯进出口公司（Louis Import & Export Company；Address：356 Bill St.，Chicago，USA.；Tel：000190-5438；Fax：000190-5439；Email：liec@hotmail.com）达成了出口 5,000 台电风扇的交易。现在，圣诞节将至，请致函该公司，给予节日祝福。

注意信中务必包含以下内容:
(1) 感谢对方在过去一年的支持,希望未来一年事业如滚雪球般发展。
(2) 希望未来一年充满了温暖、平和、幸福。
(3) 最后,对方需要询问产品信息,请与我方联系,不胜感激。

Part Ⅰ Introduction

在对外贸易中,每逢圣诞节、新年、春节、感恩节、万圣节等长假节日,我们应及时给生意往来的对象写信问候。一是为了巩固双方的友情,二是为了促进未来的长期合作。写信时措词要生动、适当,既要防止夸张,又要防止呆板。

关于问候的函电主要涉及以下内容:

(1) 圣诞问候:对于许多西方国家而言,圣诞节是一年内的头等节日,相当于中国的农历新年。一般圣诞节前,很多客户都会开始安排放假,有些客户甚至会放长假到元旦以后的许多天。为了避免耽误工作,紧急的问题需要提早在圣诞节前跟客户确认好,同时询问一下放假的具体时间,并给予节日祝福。

(2) 新年问候:新年问候通常会跟圣诞问候放在一起,但是也有很多客户不过圣诞节,比如中东地区的人们、欧美的犹太人等,对于这类客户,只要简单地道以新年祝福就可以了。所以对于圣诞祝福或者圣诞贺卡,发送之前一定要弄清楚客户是否会过圣诞节。

(3) 春节问候:中国人的春节往往是一年中最重要的假期,对于供应商、客户、生意上往来的各类朋友,都需要告知他们你春节的放假情况,并对他们表示祝福。

(4) 感恩节问候:感恩节是美国的全国性节日,盛行于美国和加拿大。感恩节到圣诞节的这一个多月期间,美国零售业的销售额能占据全年销售额的三分之一,是商家打折的促销旺季。所以感恩节前夕,可以向美国零售商致以节日问候,预祝他生意兴隆。但必须注意,感恩节不是欧美共有,欧洲没有感恩节,千万不能向欧洲人祝贺,那是非常不礼貌的。

(5) 万圣节问候:万圣节在每年的10月31日,是西方世界的主要节日之一。万圣节起源于欧洲传统的鬼节,几个世纪以来,逐渐转化为今天的节日。每到万圣节前一天,孩子们就会穿着奇装异服,装扮成各种恐怖的形象,挨家挨户敲门要糖。这一天是孩子们一年中尽情欢乐的日子。万圣节前夕,给客户道一声祝福,或者送给他的孩子一些小礼物,效果都是非常好的。

(6) 长假问候:海外客户每年除了公共假期外,还会留出一定的时间休年假,跟家人一起旅行或者好好休息一阵子。欧美客户一般会选择7、8月最热的时候,去中东、马尔代夫、摩纳哥等地旅行。时间短的可能一周,长的甚至会达两个月。工作上的事情,最好不要在休假期间打扰客户。假期结束后,与客户联系工作的同时,也要适当问候一下他假期的情况。

Part Ⅱ Letter Writing Guide

1. For letters of greetings for Christmas 圣诞问候

(1) Asking about vacation time.

(2) Expressing your thanks for the support in the past year.

(3) Expressing blessings.

2. For letters of greetings for New Year 新年问候

(1) Informing the other party of your office hours.

(2) Contacting anytime for inquiry.

(3) Expressing New Year's greetings.

3. For letters of greetings for Spring Festival 春节问候

(1) Informing the other party of your vacation time.

(2) Informing the other party of your office hours.

(3) Expressing wishes.

4. For letters of greetings for Thanksgiving Day 感恩节问候

(1) Wishing a prosperous business.

(2) Expressing wishes.

5. For letters of greetings Halloween 万圣节问候

(1) Gifts for the children.

(2) Expressing wishes.

6. For letters of greetings for holiday 长假问候

(1) Asking when to return.

(2) Expressing reasons for inquiry.

(3) Expressing wishes.

Part Ⅲ Sample Letters

1. Greetings for Christmas

Dear Amy,

Glad to hear that your company will be closed from December 22nd to 29th for

Christmas holiday.

Thanks for your support in the past year and I wish you, your colleagues & your family of this optimal holiday!

Best regards,

Teddy

 Notes

1. wholehearted [ˌhəʊlˈhɑːtid] *adj.* 全心全意的；由衷的，真心的，用来强调后面的 congratulations(祝贺)或 greetings(祝福)。

   e.g. Please take my wholehearted congratulations to Jimmy, for his promotion.
   请给吉米带去我由衷的祝贺,祝贺他升职。

   e.g. Despite our hard work and wholehearted enthusiasm, we finally lost the order from Disney.

   e.g. 尽管我们努力工作,满腔热情,但最终还是没有拿下迪斯尼的订单。

2. optimal [ˈɒptɪməl] *adj.* 最优的,最佳的

   e.g. By use of novel approaches and techniques, the optimal error estimates are obtained.

   通过引入新的证明方法和技巧,得到了最优误差估计。

3. best regards 最好的问候

   e.g. My best regards to Mary.

   请转达我对玛丽的最好祝愿。

2. Greetings for New Year

Dear Antony,

Please note that I will not be in office during January 1st to 4th, due to the New Year holiday.

For any questions, please call my mobile or send me short message.

Happy New Year! Hope it brings you more success and happiness!

Beat regards,

Christina

 Notes

1. "I wish you a happy new year"和"I wish you Happy New Year"意思是否相同?

   这两句话意思完全不同,不能乱用,一定小心。I wish you a happy new year. 这句话的意思是祝你新的一年快乐,侧重点是一整年,而不是新年的一天或者几天的假期。

   I wish you Happy New Year. 这句话的意思是祝你新年快乐,没有侧重一整年,而是指新年这个假期。在地道的英文表达里,这个用法非常罕见,似乎在语感上也有所欠缺,还不如简单的一句 Happy New Year 来得直接。

3. Greetings for Spring Festival

Dear All,

Our office will be closed during the Chinese New Year holiday period from February 8th to 15th. And we will resume work on 16th.

Any pending cases will be disposed after February 16th.

Wishing you all a happy new year!

Best regards,

Eileen

 Notes

1. Spring Festival 和 Chinese New Year 是否同义?

   可以理解为近义,两者都表示中国的农历新年,也就是春节。但有的时候,Spring Festival 还可以表示农历的"正月初一"。

   如果是表示春节假期,Spring Festival 可以单独表达,而 Chinese New Year 后面就需要加上单词 holiday。

2. resume ['rezjumei] n. 摘要,概述,概要;简历 [ri'zju:m] v. 重新开始;(中断后)继续; 恢复席位/地位/职位

   e.g. Send your resume with a cover letter that is specific to that particular job.
   寄出你的简历并附上一份针对那个特定工作岗位的附函。

   e.g. The search is expected to resume early today.
   预计搜寻工作会于今天早些时候重新开始。

225

e.g. The post office has promised to resume first class mail delivery to the area on Friday.

邮局承诺于星期五恢复对这个地区第一类邮件的递送。

3. pending cases 未决案件

e.g. The cement company's liability, including its settlement of the other pending cases, came to $710,000.

水泥公司赔偿责任，包括它的其他案件的清偿，达到71万美元。

4. Greetings for Thanksgiving Day

Dear Coco,

Thanksgiving Day is coming. On behalf of all staff in our company, I wish you a huge retail in the holiday season of Thanksgiving Day & Christmas.

Good luck to you all!

Best regards,

Aaron

Notes

1. Thanksgiving Day（感恩节）的由来是什么？

感恩节的历史可以追溯到17世纪，当时在英国受到迫害的清教徒们逃离英国本土，漂洋过海来到美洲大陆，许多人都死在途中或目的地。这个时候，美洲土著印第安人给这些活下来的移民提供了生活必需品，帮助并教会他们生存。所以感恩节的由来，一大部分是为了感谢印第安人的慷慨赠与和帮助。

从19世纪开始，感恩节就确定为每年11月第四个礼拜的周四，在美国是一个相当传统且有着悠久历史的节日。这一天是美国人家人团聚和举国欢庆的日子，有点类似于中国人的中秋节。

感恩节仅适用于美国和加拿大，跟欧洲人是没有关系的，欧洲人民不会去感谢远在大西洋彼岸的印第安人，所以欧洲没有感恩节，也不会有感恩节假期。对欧洲客户致以感恩节的问候，是非常不礼貌甚至会适得其反的！

在美国，感恩节和圣诞节这两个假期挨得很近，这期间也是美国人一年中的购物旺季，很多商场和百货公司都会选择在这个时候通过打折和促销来吸引消费者。不论消费者是为节日做准备也好，或是购买亲朋好友之间的赠礼也罢，对商家而言，消费者这段时间都是一个很好的销售季节。

2. on behalf of 代表某人，作为某人的代言人

    e.g. He spoke on behalf of all the members of the faculty and staff.
    他代表全体教职员工讲了话。

    e.g. On behalf of everyone here I want to thank you for your help.
    我代表在场的各位感谢你对我们的帮助。

5. Greetings for Halloween

Dear Eva,

Have you prepared the sales for Halloween pumpkin? Hope all the items have already been set up in the stores.

An updated sample was sent to you by FedEx, maybe you could try it next year. I bought some interesting Halloween gifts from Toys R Us, and put them into the sample parcel. The tracking number is ×××. Please help to transfer them to your kids.

                                                        Best regards,

                                                        Stephy

 Notes

1. 万圣节是怎么来的？

    万圣节和感恩节不同，不仅是美洲大陆的节日，也是澳大利亚和新西兰及欧洲国家的重要节日。在西方，11月1日是传统意义上的"All Hallow's Day"（天下圣徒之日），而前夜就是Halloween，和圣诞节前夜的Christmas Eve是同样的道理。

    万圣节起源于古英伦三岛的凯尔特人（Celtics），在他们的信仰里，新的一年从每年的11月1日开始，而死亡之神会带领鬼魂们在10月31日晚上重返人间，寻找替身。所以他们点燃火炬，用奇装异服装扮自己，让鬼魂们认不出自己以逃过灾难。后来，万圣节就慢慢从不列颠和欧洲诸国，传到美洲大陆和大洋洲等地的英国殖民地和自治领。

    如今，万圣节已逐渐褪去宗教色彩，转变为一个让孩子们欢乐的节日。孩子们可以穿各种衣服，装扮成任何想要的样子，如僵尸、吸血鬼、恶魔等，挨家挨户敲门要糖，尽情欢乐。

2. FedEx [ˈfɛˈdɛks] 联邦快递（国际性速递集团）

    联邦快递（FedEx）是一家国际性速递集团，提供隔夜快递、地面快递、重型货物运送、文件复印及物流服务，总部设于美国田纳西州孟菲斯，隶属于美国联邦快递集团（FedEx Corp）。

3. Toys "R" Us 玩具反斗城

玩具反斗城(英语Toys "R" Us,在其标志中的写法是Toys "Я" Us)是全球最大的玩具及婴幼儿用品零售商,通过整合各类品牌,向消费者提供全方位及一站式购物。

在美国和波多黎各有873家玩具"反"斗城和宝宝"反"斗城的店铺,在其他国家拥有600多家店铺,并在35个国家和地区有超过140家特许专卖店。

玩具"反"斗城总部设在美国新泽西州韦恩,在全球约有70,000名员工。为使顾客购物更方便,玩具"反"斗城每间分店都会分为以下7个主题区域,不同区域都有不同的主题颜色,每个区都乐趣无穷。

(1) 反斗一族:男孩的动感地带。区内有超级英雄模型、手办模型、电影和卡通主角、遥控车、模型车、玩具卡车、玩具飞机、玩具直升机、玩具组合等。

(2) 女孩至爱:女孩梦想成真。区内有不同类型的洋娃娃,包括时装造型娃娃、婴儿娃娃、绒毛玩具、洋娃娃服装、首饰、玩具组合、角色扮演玩具等。

(3) 合家欢游戏:适合一家人玩乐。区内有最齐备的纸板游戏、家庭乐游戏、策略游戏和其他游戏。

(4) 益智玩具:最多种类的教育和学习玩具,最优良的教育玩具,有助于孩子的发展和早期学习。积木、手工艺用品、电子学习辅助玩具和软件、泥胶、拼图、互动玩具、科学玩具、光学玩具、显微镜、上学用品应有尽有。

(5) 潮流新领域:热卖的电子产品、收藏玩具、游戏、DVD/VCD影碟、数码影碟,适合任何年龄。区内有Xbox、Playstation、掌上游戏机,还有最新颖的电子游戏和软件。

(6) 户外运动站:球类、自行车、游戏屋、滑梯、电动踏行车、折叠踏板车、攀爬组合、冲浪板、滑水板、风筝、水上玩具、沙滩玩具、水池玩具、园艺玩具、环境游戏……每一件都给你无穷的户外乐趣。

(7) BabiesRus:精选的初生婴儿用品、婴儿安全及护理产品及配件,最齐备的婴幼儿玩具及早教玩具。婴儿手推车、提篮、汽车椅、加高椅、摇篮车、婴儿床、游戏床、安全栏、婴儿食品和奶粉、婴儿床玩具、沐浴玩具、音乐玩具、摇铃,样样具备。

6. Greetings for Holiday

Dear Clair,

I'm so glad to hear that you will be on holiday to Monaco next week.

When will you come back to office? We'd like to check with you for the pending licensed order for Chevrolet.

Have a nice trip and enjoy your holiday!

Spenser

Notes

1. 如何用英语形容一个不休假的工作狂?

   工作狂在欧美地区是一个中性词,一方面赞扬某人在工作上的努力,另一方面也觉得某人相对古板且不懂得休闲。英语中有两个近义词,一个是 workaholic,另一个是 ergasiomania。相对来说,前者更有赞扬的褒义,后者的狂热程度更深,给人的印象不太好。因为 aholic 理解为"沉迷于……的人",而 mania 这个单词的意思则偏向于"狂热、狂躁"。

   e.g. The guy is a workaholic. He works all year around without a holiday.
   这个家伙是个工作狂。他一年到头只工作不休假。

   e.g. My boss is an absolutely ergasiomania, who works from dawn till midnight and never gives himself a weekend.
   我的老板是个地地道道的工作狂,每天一早工作到半夜,连周末都从来不休息。

2. Monaco [ˈmɒnəkəʊ] 摩纳哥

   摩纳哥公国(法语:La Principauté de Monaco,英语:The Principality of Monaco),简称摩纳哥,是位于欧洲的一个城邦国家,是欧洲四个公国之一(另三个是列支敦士登、卢森堡、安道尔),也是世界第二小的国家(面积最小的是梵蒂冈),总面积为 1.98 平方千米。

   摩纳哥地处法国南部,除了靠地中海的南部海岸线之外,全境北、西、东三面皆由法国包围。摩纳哥主要是由摩纳哥旧城和随后建立起来的周遭地区组成。作为世界上人口最稠密的国家之一,摩纳哥也是一个典型的微型国家。

   早期腓尼基人在此建立城堡,1297 年起由格里马尔迪家族统治,1338 年成为独立公国,1525 年受西班牙保护,1793 年受法国保护,1861 年独立。

   摩纳哥是一个高度发达的资本主义国家,国民极其富裕,同时也是世界上人均收入最高的国家之一。摩纳哥经济发达,主要以博彩、旅游和银行业为主,公国在服务业和小型的、高附加值的、无污染的工业的多种经营上进行了成功的开发。

   摩纳哥虽然面积不到 2 平方千米,但是它既有中世纪风格的街道和皇宫,也有著名的大赌场及其周边的豪华酒店,还有热带植物园和海洋博物馆。著名的网球公开赛以及在市中心举行的无与伦比的一级方程式汽车大赛都会令这个小国成为举世关注的热点。

3. Chevrolet [ˌʃɛvrəˈleɪ] 雪佛兰

   该品牌始创于 1911 年,作为深受主流中坚人群喜爱的国际汽车品牌,雪佛兰以真实自然、年轻心态、充满自信、乐观向上、富有创意的品牌个性,将人性化科技和可靠品质的产品带给中国消费者。

Part Ⅳ　Useful Expressions and Sentences

Expressions

1. Christmas [ˈkrisməs] n. 圣诞节
2. Thanksgiving Day 感恩节
3. Halloween [ˌhæləʊˈiːn] n. 万圣节前夕
4. Chinese New Year 春节（简写为 CNY）
5. Spring Festival 春节
6. wholehearted 全心全意的，由衷的
7. Season's Greetings! 圣诞快乐!
8. best regards 最好的问候
9. resume [ˈrezjumei] n. 摘要；概述；概要；简历 [riˈzjuːm] v. 重新开始；(中断后)继续；恢复席位/地位/职位
10. on behalf of 代表某人，作为某人的代言人

Typical Sentences

1. Please enjoy your holiday and celebrate the Christmas.
   请好好享受你的假期，欢度圣诞。
2. We hope you will get everything your heart desires.
   祝您心想事成。
3. May success and happiness in the coming new year!
   祝您在新的一年里有更多的成功与欢乐!
4. On behalf of our sales department, I wish you all a happy new year.
   我代表我们公司业务部全体同事，祝你们新年快乐。
5. All the goods will be shipped before the CNY holiday.
   所有的货都会在春节前出运。
6. Please settle the payment before our CNY holiday. Thank you!
   请在我们春节放假前付款。谢谢!
7. Do you have promotion plan before Thanksgiving Day?
   你们在感恩节前夕有促销计划吗?
8. Shall we have Thanksgiving dinner together?
   我们能一起共进感恩节晚餐吗?
9. Do you have interest to buy some Halloween costume?

请问您是否有兴趣采购一些万圣节装束？

10. I remember the first time I told you I was going on vacation.

我记得我第一时间就告诉过你我要去休假了。

Part Ⅴ   Practical Training

 1. Translate the following English into Chinese.

(1) Christmas

(2) Thanksgiving Day

(3) Halloween

(4) Chinese New Year

(5) Spring Festival

(6) wholehearted

(7) Season's Greetings!

(8) best regards

(9) resume

(10) on behalf of

(11) Please enjoy your holiday and celebrate the Christmas.

(12) We hope you will get everything your heart desires.

(13) May success and happiness in the coming New Year!

(14) On behalf of our sales department，I wish you all a happy new year.

(15) All the goods will be shipped before the CNY holiday.

(16) Please settle the payment before our CNY holiday. Thank you!

(17) Do you have promotion plan before Thanksgiving Day?

(18) Shall we have Thanksgiving dinner together?

(19) Do you have interest to buy some Halloween costume?

(20) I remember the first time I told you I was going on vacation.

 2. Translate the following Chinese into English.

(1) 祝你一切顺心。

(2) 请接受我们由衷的圣诞祝福。

(3) 请好好享受您的假期，欢度圣诞。

(4) 我亲爱的朋友，祝你新年快乐！

(5) 祝您农历新年假期快乐！

(6) 恐怕最后一个订单要在春节后出货了。

(7) 由于春节期间劳动力缺乏，很抱歉通知你，货需要延期三个航次。

(8) 春节前是我们最忙的时候。

(9) 感恩节快要到了。

(10) 很明显今年感恩节假期的销售情况会非常棒。

(11) 我计划去梅西百货和百思买逛逛，找一些有意思的东西。

(12) 请参加我们下周一在香港兰桂坊举办的万圣节酒会。

(13) 我们会在香港半岛酒店举行万圣节晚宴。

(14) 万圣节是你的孩子们的节日。

(15) 万圣节期间你打算如何销售？

(16) 我正在巴厘岛休年假，下周二会回去工作。

(17) 度假的人们喜欢7月去迪拜。

(18) 今天是英国的银行休假日。

(19) 他那时候在度假，我们在这之前没有收到过任何关于船期方面的确认。

(20) 愿你所有的圣诞梦想都成真！

3. Choose the best answer.

(1) Wishing you a song ____ your heart ____ Christmas and blessings all year long.
    A. in, in   B. at, at   C. in, at   D. on, in

(2) Wishing you peace, joy and happiness ____ Christmas and the coming year.
    A. through   B. at   C. in   D. on

(3) Warm greetings and best wishes ____ Christmas and the New Year!
    A. of   B. at   C. with   D. for

(4) Thinking ____ you and wishing you a beautiful Christmas season.
    A. with   B. of   C. about   D. in

(5) It seems that Christmas time is here once again, and it is time again to bring ____ the New Year.
    A. to   B. with   C. about   D. in

(6) May Christmas and the New Year be filled ____ happiness for you.
    A. in   B. of   C. with   D. to

(7) A Christmas greeting and good wishes ____ you who is thought ____ all the year through.
    A. to, about   B. to, with   C. for, about   D. for, with

(8) A Christmas greeting ____ cheer you ____ your daughters.
    A. to, from   B. to, for
    C. for, from   D. for, for

(9) Wishing you all the blessings ____ a beautiful Christmas season.
    A. with   B. for   C. at   D. of

(10) ____ greetings and ____ wishes for happiness and ____ luck in the coming year.
   A. Best, warm, good
   B. Warm, best, good
   C. Good, warm, best
   D. Best, good, warm

Reference
参考文献

[1] 黄丽威.外贸函电与单证[M].北京:高等教育出版社,2006.

[2] 景凯文,凌恩英.商务电子邮件写作大全[M].北京:北京语言大学出版社,2011.

[3] 李宏亮.国际商务函电[M].北京:对外经济贸易大学出版社,2008.

[4] 廖英.实用外贸英语函电[M].武汉:华中科技大学出版社,2005.

[5] 刘崇,曲丽君.纺织服装外贸英语函电[M].2版.北京:中国纺织出版社,2013.

[6] 綦颖,王菲,钱福东.国际贸易函电[M].北京:北京理工大学出版社,2009.

[7] 隋思忠.外贸英语函电[M].大连:东北财经大学出版社,2004.

[8] 万婷.新编外贸函电[M].济南:山东大学出版社,2018.

[9] 王俊.商务英语函电[M].北京:对外经济贸易大学出版社,2011.

[10] 王乃彦.对外经贸英语函电[M].北京:对外经济贸易大学出版社,2010.

[11] 王兴孙,张春鉎,邬孝煜.新编进出口英语函电[M].北京:外语教学与研究出版社,2012.

[12] 王珏.商务写作与外贸函电[M].北京:中国人民大学出版社,2017.

[13] 吴思乐,胡秋华.世纪商务英语外贸函电[M].3版.大连:大连理工大学出版社,2015.

[14] 徐俊.外贸英语函电实务[M].北京:中国商业出版社,2016.

[15] 毅冰.十天搞定外贸函电[M].北京:中国海关出版社,2012.

[16] 易露露,刘洁,尤彧聪.外贸英语函电[M].北京:清华大学出版社,2008.

[17] 伊辉春.新编外贸英语函电[M].北京:化学工业出版社,2016.

[18] 尹小莹,杨润辉.外贸英语函电:商务英语应用文写作[M].西安:西安交通大学出版社,2011.

[19] 张静,张晓云.外贸英语函电[M].北京:高等教育出版社,2018.

[20] 赵萱,郑仰成.实用英语应用文写作教程[M].北京:高等教育出版社,2011.